Kachcheri Bureaucracy in Sri Lanka: The Culture and Politics of Accessibility

Namika Raby

Foreign and Comparative Studies/South Asian Series, No. 10
Maxwell School of Citizenship and Public Affairs
Syracuse University
1985

Library of Congress Cataloging in Publication Data

Raby, Namika, 1946-
    Kachcheri bureaucracy in Sri Lanka.

    (Foreign and comparative studies/South Asian
series ; no. 10)
    Bibliography: p.
    Includes index.
    1. State governments--Sri Lanka Provinces.
2. Bureaucracy--Sri Lanka--Provinces. I. Title.
II. Series: Foreign and comparative studies. South
Asian series ; no. 10.
JQ659.A88R33 1985   354.9'301   85-11439
ISBN 0-915984-88-1

To my parents
and to George and Leila

TABLE OF CONTENTS

NOTE ON TRANSLITERATION

Sinhala terms are transliterated according to established conventions in the literature. Many such terms cannot be readily translated into a single English gloss. In this work a single gloss epitomizes the use of a term in a given context.

ACKNOWLEDGMENTS

With much pleasure and deep appreciation, I should like to identify the agencies and individuals who have made this book possible. The field research on which it is based was conducted in Sri Lanka under a doctoral fellowship from the Social Science Research Council and the American Council of Learned Societies. Many individuals helped to shape the original dissertation, above all my doctoral chairman, Donald F. Tuzin. The transition from dissertation to book was undertaken with the guiding presence of F.G. Baily, who helped me recast the original materials and painstakingly read through my revisions. Over the years, Gananath Obeyesekere has been both mentor and friend, giving me the benefit of his advice in bringing some of the issues addressed in this work into sharper focus, and, along with Ranjini Obeyesekere, checking on the transliteration of Sinhala terms. Michael Meeker has generously lent his analytical skills in directing me to search for further meaning in my data. On handling a subject that is truly interdisciplinary, I have been aided by individuals in other disciplines; here I must mention the sharp and relentless intellect of David Laitin, who as a political scientist challenged me to seek fresh insights on the subject.

To the people of Ganvälla, Sri Lanka, I have ties other than those of anthropologist-observer, and I cannot sufficiently emphasize their many acts of kindness during the course of my research. The Sri Lanka Ministry of Home Affairs, in granting me permission to conduct this study, made it all possible. At the Ganvälla kachcheri, particularly in the office of the AGA, the warmth and willing cooperation of the officials helped me to successfully conclude my research. In order to maintain their anonymity I have used fictitious names for places and persons associated with this office. In Sri Lanka, I was fortunate in being able to interview Mr. Bradman Weerakoon, who, amidst a busy schedule, took the time and effort to share with me his insights and experience, specifically on the colonial GA and his contemporary counterpart.

The patience and encouragement of my husband, George M. Scott, Jr., helped me through the tedium of revision. Michele Wenzel, with patience and good cheer, typed this manuscript. Finally, I am grateful to Mary Beth Ritter for her work in editing the final manuscript.

CHAPTER 1

The Problem and the Setting

The forts in Ceylon[1] were largely the creation of the
Dutch. Subsequently, in British times, they became the locus of
kachcheri[*] administration. Protected on all sides by the sea,
river and ramparts, the Ganvälla kachcheri is located inside
one of the two forts built in Ganvälla during the late 18th
century. Outside lies the noise and confusion of the bus stop
and the market place, peopled by vendors, snake charmers, palm
readers and native medicine men. By contrast, the immediate
precincts of the fort are quiet, as befits the staid routine of
bureaucratic administration. At the entrance to the fort there
is a Methodist church, while to the right stand the barracks of
an army regiment. Beyond these, under the shade of a banyan
tree, lies the kachcheri. The main buildings are at least 100
years old, with adobe floors, a Spanish-style tiled roof, and
pillared verandahs interconnecting the buildings. Office
furniture belongs in style to the British era; so do office
techniques. Computerized office methods are absent, and clerks
and minor employees are the mainstay of the system.

The focus of this book is the regional bureaucracy
(kachcheri) in an administrative district[2], here called
Ganvälla, in the low country of Sri Lanka.[3] The kachcheri
is headed by an official called the Government Agent (GA), who
is a high-ranking member of the Sri Lanka Administrative
Service. The GA and his subordinates are the representatives of

---

[*]In everyday language, kachcheri refers to district
administration, but in practice the three levels of district,
division, and village are so interconnected through the
supervisory and delegated authority of the GA that, in this
book, I refer to all three levels as the kachcheri bureaucracy.

the central government at the district level, and are required
to implement policies of social welfare and economic
development. The district is divided into 10 divisions, called
either DRO (Divisional Revenue Office) or AGA (Assistant
Government Agent) divisions. My field research was carried out
in one of these divisions.

The Problem

Secular rationalization, the foundation of Max Weber's
philosophy of history, is epitomized in modern bureaucratic
organizations, which are formal and impersonal. Weber considers
this process of rationalization to be inevitable and
irreversible, and to be accompanied by a change in human
attitudes and ways of thinking. The result is "disenchantment
of the world." The ultimate and sublime values of society
retreat from public life into the "transcendental realm of
mystic life or into the brotherliness of direct and personal
human relations....It is not accidental that only within the
smallest and intimate circles, in personal human situations, in
pianissimo, that something is pulsating that corresponds to the
prophetic pneuma, which in former times swept through the great
communities like a firebrand, welding them together" (Weber
1973:155).

Allowing that bureaucracy is the product of rationalization,
scientific technology, and industrial society, studies even in
such societies, notably in the United States,[*] reveal the
existence of personalism within organizations otherwise
structured around principles of formalism and impersonalism.

---

[*]For example, Roethlisberger and Dickson 1939; Blau 1963;
Pressman and Wildavsky 1974; Bailey 1977; and Britan and
Chibrink 1980.

This personalism derives from two sources: first, officials must interpret organizational policy in the course of implementing it; second, informal networks of social relationships develop between members of an organization and, at times, between them and their clients. In either case, Weber's "disenchantment" is countered by a personalization supposedly absent from the public realm.

In transitional societies such as Sri Lanka, the nature of this personalization is influenced by the norms of the sociocultural environment within which the bureaucratic system is embedded. This study is an analysis of how an administrative bureaucracy, the kachcheri, reflects the design of Sri Lankan culture. It is a study of the politics of meaning.[4] To personalize human relationships is to make them meaningful.[5] But to personalize such relationships within a bureaucracy formally structured according to rational, impersonal principles, operating within a cultural setting based on the premise of personalization, is to make the relationships especially meaningful.

The kachcheri, during the course of its routine functioning, is viewed analytically as a source of formal and symbolic power for the official, and as an arena for political behavior (i.e., manipulation and power struggle) between official and client as expressed in both symbolic and nonsymbolic exchanges. These two aspects of the administrative system will be the subject of closer examination and analysis.

Beginning with the Assistant Government Agent, the higher ranks within the kachcheri hierarchy are designated as "staff officers," that is, those vested with executive powers. Their powers and functions are defined by the "AR and the FR," or the Administrative and Financial Regulations, respectively, supplemented by circulars released by the Government Treasury from time to time. The AR and the FR are specifically defined documents, but they are at least 100 years old. Thus, in interpreting these regulations to suit contemporary situations, the official exercises considerable discretionary power. The "Treasury Circulars," on the other hand, are issued to cover unforeseen circumstances, or an organizational alteration of the administrative machinery, without recourse to parliamentary legislation.[6] The ambiguity of these circulars confers additional discretionary authority on the staff officer.

The clerks and the grama sevakas [rural service officers, hereafter called GS] belong to nonstaff grades; they have authority only insofar as it is delegated to them by a staff officer, notably the AGA. The latter's countersignature is required in order to validate decisions made by these officials. Nevertheless, the powers and duties allocated to a clerk in charge of a particular type of task, as well as the functions of the grama sevakas, are his perquisites of office and the countersignature is a formality. Hence, it could be concluded that all of these officials derive their powers of office, either directly or indirectly, from the administrative system.

The formal power of the administrator, derived from the AR, the FR, and the Treasury Circulars, is expressed in a symbolic idiom of status here referred to as the "seat." The tremendous, historically derived cultural resonance of the position of administrator gives the position symbolic significance, which is expressd in the concept of the "seat."

The Seat as a Symbol

When an official speaks of his seat, he refers to the chair he occupies behind his desk. He conducts his official duties from this position. If he is not in his seat, he is not available to the public, whether he is in a different part of the office, in consultation, or chatting with a colleague. There is reluctance on the part of an official to relay a phone message to a fellow official who is not in his seat. In his eyes, to relay a message to an official who is in his seat is part of his duty, while to do so for an official who is out of his seat signifies an act of friendship where none might exist. To sit in another's seat is to invite anger and ridicule, and signifies an act of usurpation or challenge to one's authority. While these are manifest meanings often adduced by the officials themselves, one must go beyond them to discover the larger social meanings attached to the seat.

First, a seat indicates positioning in a caste-based society such as Sri Lanka's; a lower seat is offered to a member of a lower caste, while his caste superior occupies a higher seat. The lowest in the caste hierarchy may not have any seat, and instead may squat in the presence of a superior.[7] At the level of social-personal significance, the seat as a symbol in a caste-based society is "a mechanism for the development of selfhood and for tackling the perennial problems of human existence" (Cohen 1974:x-xi). A fragile link is maintained between the person-occupant of the position and the symbolic significance he attaches to the seat. The position, power, and prestige signified by the seat is synonymous with the position, power, and prestige of its occupant. Then, to occupy another's seat is to violate one's notion of self which, within the context of a status-based society, must remain inviolate. It follows that the seat then becomes a cultural symbol which also has personal meaning.[8]

This seat as a symbol is not the weapon of the formally powerless; instead, it formally confers considerable power on the individual occupant. However, given the symbolic content of the officer-client dyad, the official must manipulate the power resources symbolized by his seat in order to be a man of consequence in the community. He simplifies his position by distinguishing the "known faces" among his clients, and manipulates culturally acceptable idioms to do so. However, in the face of unlimited, inconvenient, and at times impossible demands by the "known face," he must still walk a tightrope. When he is unable to do so, a situation described as "cannot say no," he loses face; this condition is described vividly by the phrases palvenavā [to stink or stagnate], and sāyama giyā [to have the paint washed off]. To fall into this condition is cause for frustration, anger, and hostility toward the one who caused it. This situation is compounded by the fact that one may not express such feelings to the source; instead, they must be contained within the bureaucratic persona. To state that this symbol is a phenomenon *sui generis* is to bypass its sociocultural significance, and to say that it is manipulated in the struggle for, and the maintenance of power between individuals (Cohen 1974:ix) is to offer an incomplete explanation. This particular case has illustrated an area which cannot be manipulated, and which causes pain. Meaning is managed (Cohen and Comaroff 1976:87-103) and to that extent, an official is in control of his interaction with a client; but when he is no longer able to impose self-selected cultural meaning, he loses control of such an interaction.

In conclusion, both a similarity and a striking contrast can be seen between the symbolic significance of the seat in the Sri Lankan kachcheri and public titles as a symbolic order for defining the person in Bali (Geertz 1973:385-89; 398-403). In Sri Lanka as in Bali, bureaucratic positions are symbolized by the seat. But unlike Bali, in Sri Lanka this does not rest on a sharp distinction between the domestic and public sectors. Rather, there is a carry-over of individual and familiar concerns into the public sphere of the bureaucracy. According to Geertz (Ibid., p. 386), "For truly public men in Bali, other aspects of personhood -- individual character, birth order, kinship relations, procreative status and prestige rank -- take, symbolically at least, a secondary position...they have sacrificed their true selves to their role...their role is the essence of their true selves." Personality is thus concealed behind the ready-made identities of position. The anonymity of individuals with whom one is in daily contact is maintained by dampening the intimacy implicit in face-to-face relations through ceremony. This attempts to lock "the more creatural aspects of the human condition -- individual, spontaneity, perishability, emotionality, vulnerability -- from sight" (Ibid., p. 399).

In Sri Lanka, the officials as public figures use their positions as vehicles to express individual and familiar aspects of personhood. Instead of sacrificing their true selves to their role, they express their true selves through their role. Personality is expressed rather than concealed behind identities of position. However, as in Bali, there is also anonymity in face-to-face relations through the bureaucratic persona. For the official, this is necessary in order to maintain his social prestige and esteem. He must be a sāhena nilādariyek [respectable officer] in the eyes of clients and fellow officials, and must not be too accessible to them. However, an official's self-image expressed through his position must find validation in community interaction. If he is too accessible, he will lose face in the eyes of the community; but he must be accessible in order to gain its respect.

Bureaucracy as a Political Arena

As an arena for political behavior, the structural framework of the kachcheri admits two sets of participants: the officials and the clients. In practice, within its organization dimension,[9] there are actually three sets: the official, the client, and the politician vis-a-vis his role as client. The structure provides the goals (summarized as welfare and development), the rules and procedures of who is eligible, and how one sets about attaining these goals. This structural framework ie established by the political system. With the official as the nexus, the kachcheri in fact becomes a wide-open arena where the range of goals to be achieved is broad, the demands upon its services outweigh its resources, the bureaucratic procedures are complicated, and many diverse

cultural themes are used as tactical weapons by the
participants.

For the official, his formal powers must find expression and
validation in accessibility through personalized social
relationships with clients. He must negotiate a balance between
being a good man and an efficient administrator, and in the
interests of both, he must draw the line between being
accessible and too accessible. His refuge is the bureaucratic
persona. A successful official must have the personal touch; he
must step out of this persona and create community good will for
himself. In this process he distinguishes between certain
categories of clients -- referred to as the "known face," the
"unknown helpless," and the "unknown face" -- and permits them
access to him on moral, ethical, and transactional grounds,
respectively.

Moral ties spring from the face-to-face community setting
with its emphasis on kinship, village affiliation, and
friendship, all expressed in the idiom of kinship. Ethical
considerations emerge from the cultural value of humanity and
the Buddhist ideals of compassion and merit. Transactional
relationships are based on the cultural expectations of
reciprocity through commensality, symbolizing equality in a
caste-based society, the traditional practice of exchanging
goods for services, and an extended use of the customary
practice of gift-giving. This results in a situation where
officials as members of a formally modern bureaucratic system
"bend backwards and forwards at the same time" (Ibid., p. 320),
thereby accommodating (instead of replacing) tradition within a
modern structure.

The accessibility of an official based on ethical
considerations does not pose a problem for him. In this case,
the nature of the request is limited and clients have adequate
justification -- documentary and verbal -- for making a
request. Helping a client who is obviously an inferior in
status is not a threat to the official in this type of

interaction. On the contrary, it enhances his social prestige and esteem and ultimately, his self-image. However, this is of little consequence in comparison to an official's interaction (based on moral considerations) with his face-to-face community, which serves as his reference group.

In constrast, official accessibility based on personal moral considerations poses a dilemma for the official. Given that he must be accessible to them, he still cannot and may not (given the nature and scope of their demands) accede to each request. Neither is he able to stop the flow of such requests. In order to retain his prestigious public image, he must help them. Repeated requests for help, which would involve bending the rules too often, pose a threat to his position in the bureaucracy. But to refuse help to a "known face" (which in this case is construed as inability to help) results in embarrassment and loss of face for the official, and may produce a negative self-image. If the official cannot help a "known face" himself, and therefore is forced to seek the help of his peers, such a request may be turned down by the latter; this too results in embarrassment and loss of face. This is cause for resentment, especially in the case of the "known face" who is not considered legitimate, such as the political monk.

With the "unknown," the official need not walk a tightrope. He is in control of the transaction, and decides on the extent of his accessibility. This depends on the demeanor of the client, or on the monetary gains received or anticipated from the transaction. The unknown-aggressive client, by violating the rules of initiating a transaction in an acceptable manner, challenges the position and authority of the official and thus the values associated with personhood. By emphasizing (and at times by overemphasizing) the normative requirements of the bureaucracy, and by exercising his own discretion, the official can keep this client at the back of the queue for a while.

The mudalāli [entrepreneur] is allowed access because of his ability to make a transaction on the principle of balanced exchange of goods for services. While the political monk evokes the hostility of the official, the mudalāli evokes his disdain. The ideals of the monk role are based on abstinence from participation in the mundane world for self-gain, and the monk who violates this loses his right to respectful consideration from the official. The mudalāli, on the other hand, is given consideration, despite the disdain visited upon the noveau riche, because of continued contact with their mode of livelihood. Clients who gain access to an official through a gift do so only in the lowest echelons of the administration. Transactions are negotiated and completed surreptitiously, and become a direct and self-terminating exchange of goods or cash in return for services. In offering a gift, the client recognizes and validates the official's power and authority in that particular transaction.

The "unknowns" who gain access to the official through the use of coercion provide a study in contrast to the "known face" and the other cases of the "unknown" discussed above. Here the official does not obtain self-gratification for helping them; neither can he control accessibility. Clients using force give the official no chance to refuse access. Failure to oblige may have damaging consequences for the official or his family. On the other hand, obliging such clients may win for the official, and for his family, the protection of these clients within the community.

The official steps out of his bureaucratic persona for the "unknown-helpless" because he does not fear that the latter may embarrass his for being too accessible. He trusts the "known faces" and therefore becomes accessible to them, and he hopes that they will not embarass him by making undue demands. In giving controlled access to the mudalāli as well as to clients using gifts, and in denying access to the unknown-aggressive, the official is in control of the transaction and therefore does not risk the possibility of losing face or suffering embarrassment. In making a transaction with clients who use coercion, the official saves himself from physical harm and consequent damage to his self-image. In the final analysis, the official and the "known" or "unknown" clients who gain access to him on ethical, moral, or transactional grounds interact as members of a face-to-face community bound together by ties of reciprocity.

Access to the official rather than access to the service is the subject of discussion. A client may approach an official whom he knows personally, knowing that this official is not in charge of a particular task, but expecting him to intercede with the official who is in charge of this task. A client who cannot gain access to an official may not obtain goods or services as speedily as those who do, but he may still succeed by meeting the normative requirements of the administrative system. He fills out the appropriate application and he follows the required procedure.

In a culture which is not as oriented toward the clock as those of industrial societies, time in its own right as a factor in access (Schwartz 1975) is less significant.[10] The social worth of a client (Ibid., pp. 13-46) enters into the transaction, but this is not an index of the value of his time spent waiting, but rather of his value as an ally in the community in a symbolic, ornamental sense.

To conclude, the theme of access to the official is completed with the case of the politician. Client-official interactions are no longer transactions between situational superiors and inferiors, but between potential rivals whose separate authority, while derived from different sources, is nevertheless brought to bear upon administrative decision making. The politician attempts to gain access to the official on behalf of his supporters, or to gain access not to the official but to the power and prestige of the latter's office and so usurp that power and prestige.

The entry of local political figures into the administrative arena signals that the range of interactions anchored upon the administrator has come full circle. If the first category of interactions is moral, the latter is best described as immoral. Insofar as it is created by the political assembly at the national level, the kachcheri bureaucracy is a creature of the political system. However, once created, the ethos of its administration is one of independence through functioning under the direction of the national power structure, in this case the Ministry of Home Affairs, the cabinet and the prime minister, and ultimately the president. Actions by political figures outside this framework are interpreted by the administrators as immoral interference. Attempts at interference by local politicians, the party organizer, the MP, and the district political authority, are viewed in a similar light. Many an administrator explained that the local politician has no statutory authority for intervening in administrative routine. But these administrators are also well aware that the national political structure could confer administrative decision-making functions upon local politicians (as has happened in the case of the district political authority), or that a politician championing the cause of the masses could use his position to obtain administrative spoils. In either case, the administrator is powerless to defend or retaliate unless he himself has the backing of a politician with greater authority and influence than the one with whom he has the encounter. To the extent that a politician adopts either of these strategies, he is considered by the administrator to be both immoral and unprincipled. Bailey (1963:149) makes a distinction between the "touter," the "broker," the "boss," and the politician as they operate within the arena of the Legislative Assembly in Orissa. In the Sri Lankan case, we are dealing with the administrative rather than the legislative arena; here, the role of the politician as represented by the party organizer corresponds to Bailey's definition of the "touter," the MP to that of the "broker," and

the district political authority to that of the "boss." They
all intercede on behalf of their supporters, who must negotiate
a transaction with the administrator, but they have no access to
him through other channels. The official perceives such
interference as "telling me how to do my job." This causes
resentment. The official sees himself as losing face in the
eyes of the client who brings a chit from the party organizer or
a letter from the MP.

The district political authority, on the other hand, was
accommodated within the administrative structure through prime
ministerial fiat solely for implementing land reform and
undertaking development programs. The fact that his powers were
ill-defined provided a strategic advantage to the district
political authority, who as a result was able to spread his
sphere of influence into areas claimed by the administrator as
his by statute, and while doing so usurp the symbolic status of
the administrator, in this case the government agent (GA).

The challenges and counter-challenges between the government
agent (who was also the cooperative authority or CA), and the
political authority (PA) were publicly made in the arena of the
monthly meetings of the political authority.[11] When a
stalemate was reached, the politician publicly but indirectly
reprimanded the GA/CA through his subordinate. This caused
embarrassment and loss of face for the GA/CA (as well as for his
subordinate), and evoked the following comment from another
official: "Why must one stand up and contradict the PA, and be
unnecessarily ridiculed and lose face in public? One could take
the path of least resistance and simply carry out his orders."
As in the case of clients typed as moral, an official dealing
with clients typed as immoral faces pressure and loss of control
over the interaction, and is resentful of the embarrassment it
causes him.

In Sri Lanka, the notion of embarrassment and loss of face
is used to describe the outcome of a number of different
situations. It incorporates characteristics of what Geertz

(1973:401-2) defines as shame resulting when wrongdoing is publicly exposed, and "stage fright," which is the fear that one lacks sufficient skill or self-control to bring off a face-to-face encounter with finesse. Geertz also defines "stage fright" as the fear of *faux pas* when "the actor will show through his part and the part thus dissolve into the actor." In Sri Lanka, the official who fears to ask a peer for help on behalf of a "known face," either because he might be refused or because he fears that the "known face" will make repeated demands which he may not be able to satisfy, is suffering from the Balinese type of "stage fright." On the other hand, the fear of public reprimand or of being told how one should do one's job is different. It is not a fear of failure as an official, but rather as an individual. It offends his self-respect.

In the words of an informant, "the kachcheri is a place one goes to, from birth to death," and this statement sums up the nature and scope of its functions. It is a place which provides certificates of birth and death, and deals with the innumerable practical demands of daily life in between. The symbolic resonance of the role of administrator, the political dynamics of the administrative arena mediated through access to the official, counteract the rationalization and disenchantment of forms, files, and procedures.

The preceding cultural thematic analysis of bureaucracy, while building on existing literature on the subject, adds to it a new dimension. Taking Weber's analytical concept of the ideal type as a starting point, Blau and Scott (1962:232-34) and Katz and Eisenstadt (1965:255-59), among others, view the development of informal relations between officials and clients as deviant, a form of "debureaucratization." Katz and Danet (1966:811-22), discussing client strategies to influence an Israeli bureaucracy, state that client appeal is based more on the normative basis of the organization -- the rationale for its existence -- than on the client's ability to offer his resources

in exchange for those of the organization. Handelman
(1976:223-75) shows how a client may bring extra-organizational
indices of judgment (i.e., age, state of health, or family size)
as a means of influencing transactions within (another) Israeli
bureaucracy.

While these are studies of bureaucracy in modern industrial
societies, other writers have focused on such organizations in
traditional settings. Fallers (1965) describes the role of the
official from the perspective of conflict, as a choice between
tradition and modernity. Price (1975), in his study of
bureaucracy in Ghana, explains bureaucratic behavior in terms of
the role affiliations of the official. Heginbotham (1975)
explains administrative behavior in terms of cognitive models of
organization derived from different cultural traditions in an
Indian bureaucracy.

This book examines bureaucracy in a transitional cultural
setting. It views informal relations between officials and
clients not as deviant, but as attempts to impose meaning on a
bureaucratic apparatus based on a set of norms alien to the
cultural setting. It is a study of client strategies for
influencing the bureaucracy through its officials; it does not,
as in the cases discussed by Katz and Danet and Handelman, view
officials as representatives of the institutions in which they
work, but, like their clients, as members of a cultural
community. This requires a more lengthy discussion of the
nature of the clientele. In the work of Price, we see a linking
of social structure and process through role affiliations of the
official. The present work, taking an ethnographic approach,
also brings in the study of the nature and significance of the
clientele as the other dimension in the study of process.
Instead of viewing social relationships as emerging out of
social contact (Handelman 1976), it recognizes that, in Sri
Lanka, pre-existing social ties deriving their support from the
cultural environment are brought into play in bureaucratic
interactions. Such social ties become political resources in

the hands of both officials and clients. Thus, a social system
and a culture based on antithetical principles come to be
mediated through the behavior of individuals who are by choice
(officials) or necessity (clients) participants in the system,
and who are by circumstance participants in the culture.

The Field Situation

The bulk of the research for this study was conducted in
1976-77 under a doctoral grant from the Social Science Research
Council and the American Council of Learned Societies. But my
interest in the study of the kachcheri dates back to 1970, when
as an assistant lecturer in the Department of Sociology at the
University of Ceylon, Peradeniya, I was encouraged by the (then)
department chairman, Dr. Gananath Obeyesekere, to undertake
vacation field projects on the subject. This initial study, as
well as the subsequent research, was undertaken with the
permission of the Ministry of Home Affairs, within whose
jurisdiction the kachcheri lies. Research conducted between
1970 and 1973 was limited, both by time and by money. I chose
that particular region because I could work from home and
thereby save on expenses. I was thus not merely a native
researcher, but a hometown researcher as well.

The letter of authorization from the Ministry of Home
Affairs gave me entry into the kachcheri to carry out research
and provided me with my initial interview with the GA. But as a
hometown researcher, I was also immediately placed within the
local social network. This, coupled with my appointment at the
University of Ceylon, gave me ready and almost immediate access
into the working life of the official. I was a "known face."
In addition, my firsthand knowledge of the community proved
especially useful in collecting biographies and background
information on its members. With the single exception of an
individual who refused to be interviewed because "he does not
give any interviews," (possibly due to the politically sensitive

nature of his dealings in the community), my ties to the
community opened rather than denied me access to information.

In 1976, after spending three years in the United States,
armed with some theoretical knowledge and methodological skills
acquired there and perhaps with greater objectivity toward my
field site, I returned to Ganvälla to conduct full-time
research. Predictably, I found changes in personnel[12] and
some changes in the organization of the kachcheri. In the
interim, the focus of my research had changed from a general
study of the kachcheri organization to a study of the symbolic
and political significance of the behavior of officials and
clients as it determines access to the official. This, together
with the fact that the study used the traditional
anthropological field method of participant observation, made it
necessary to limit myself to the office of the AGA in one
administrative district, that is, to one particular divisional
office.

The theme of the work is access: that is, contact between
official and client. The divisional office, which occupies the
middle position in the district administrative hierarchy, seemed
suitable for my purposes. The district office ranks highest in
terms of executive authority, but the clients do not go there
first. If they were to do so, they would be directed either to
the divisional or village level offices. It is also possible
that a client, failing to achieve his goal through the accepted
channel, may approach the GA or his assistants, who would then
ask the divisional office to explain the reason for the
failure. Also, in performing development-oriented tasks (such
as land acquisition and alienation, and disbursing funds for
agricultural purposes), the GA makes the decisions with the
agreement of the local political leader. He then delegates the
task of implementation to the divisional office.

At the village level, the grama sevaka is simply a voice of
support (or lack of it) for tasks that are actually carried out
at the divisional level. For instance, to transfer a rice

ration book from region A to B, the work is done at the
divisional level. But a client must first obtain a letter of
certification from the GS in charge of his area of residence,
vouching for his domicile and also for his personal ownership of
the particular rice ration book. The grama sevaka also acts as
a gatherer of information about villagers[13] so that he may,
for example, authenticate whatever reasons are given when there
is a request for cement or for social assistance. He is an
important means of communication with residents, an example
being the annual house-to-house distribution of new rice ration
books. But the grama sevaka does not have independent
executive authority, so that while he deals with clients
directly and immediately, they must still go to the divisional
office to complete a transaction. In short, the divisional
office and its officer-in-charge -- the divisional revenue
officer/assistant government agent -- have both executive
authority and contact with clients.

The primary reason for my choice of the Ganvälla
divisional office rather than another in the district is that it
has the largest population in the district. Second, Ganvälla
also has the largest urban population in the district, and I
wished to see how much indigenous culture affected accessibility
in an urban setting.[14] Third, this divisional office is close
to the district office and thus especially useful for the second
part of my study, which considers both clients who are denied
access to an official and who then seek the aid of a politician,
and some others who go directly to politicians. The district
office is also relevant when, in the final chapter, we look at
the uses which politicians can make of administrators.

To carry out the study, I needed two kinds of data, archival
and field. My plan did not call for me to begin with one rather
than the other, but, two weeks after my arrival, I made my first
acquaintance with the GA of the Ganvälla kachcheri. Based on
what I considered to be a very successful interview, I plunged
directly into the task of field observation.

From the beginning the GA and his aides were aware that I had come from abroad, that I was pursuing a course of study at the University of California, and that I was writing a "book"[15] as part of my education, in order to complete a higher degree. They also knew that I was a native of the area. The GA who introduced me to the others always mentioned those features in that order. Initially, he also added, "Now gentlemen, be on your best behavior; Miss Raby is taking notes on what is going on." One could conclude that the GA making this statement preceding a formal meeting, coupled with my presence in an administrative organization where all of the executive positions were filled by males and where the secretary was the only other female, could have inhibited the behavior of at least some officials. Then, to my relief, the GA ceased drawing attention to my presence. I will return later to the question of whether my being a woman had much impact on the research.

For the next six months I concentrated on the kachcheri and the office of the AGA, the bulk of my time being spent in the latter. I interviewed the GA, the Additional GA, the latter's assistant known as AGA (Headquarters), and the other officials who make up the kachcheri. The fact that these interviews were done during office hours meant that there were frequent interruptions by the phone, by fellow officials, and by clients. This was especially true in interviews with the GA and the Additional GA. However, as I was introduced to the human interruptors, I was able to set up appointments to interview them. The clients provided some of the central cases in the research, and finally, a phone could be useful. One call, coming in the middle of an interview with the GA, led to an introduction to a well-known senior administrator, who graciously consented to a series of interviews on the GA in the colonial period and on his contemporary counterpart.

My interviews with the GA were specific as to issues, and as my research progressed, and as I needed answers to questions

which only he could supply, or clarification, I sought further
interviews with him. My initial interview with the Additional
GA focused on the form and functions of the _kachcheri_. But
since the latter had within his authority the _grama_ _sevakas_ and
land reform, subsequent interviews concerned these subjects.
Interviews with the other officials were less frequent and were
related to their areas of expertise.

I was also a participant observer at a number of formal
meetings within the _kachcheri_. These were the meetings of the
District Agricultural Committee, the District Development
Committee, and the District Political Authority (DPA). The
first two committees met infrequently (three times during my
stay), while the DPA met monthly. There was a high level of
absenteeism in the first two types of meetings, and the general
feeling among the participants was that the meetings were an
exercise in futility because the functions of these committees
had been effectively usurped by the DPA. The meetings of the
DPA were much more formal and structured than the others; a roll
call was taken, and my position was duly noted in the minutes,
though I could not understand why I was constantly referred to
as "the archeologist." Though chaired by the GA, these meetings
were essentially the politicians' show, and it was with the
DPA's oral permission, obtained in this case through the AGA,
that I was able to observe these meetings and obtain copies of
their proceedings.

My research at the AGA's office began with my interviewing
him on the form and functions of his office. It is a smaller
office in terms of space and numbers (fifteen officials), and
within the first hour, my presence was made known to the
others. Like the GA, the AGA also introduced me to the others
according to the criteria mentioned earlier, but in this case
the AGA, his successor, and the majority of the clerical and
minor staff were local residents.[16] My ties to the local
community permitted me quick rapport with them. My initial task
was interviewing each official about his or her area of work and

familiarizing myself with the documents and files that accompanied it. I started with the occupants at the front of the office and worked my way to the back. I was able to get to know each official in this manner, and I was not identified with any one person in particular. This could easily have happened if I had relied exclusively on the AGA, who was a willing informant. The strategy also prevented me from unwittingly violating informal ranking in terms of age and sex as well as formal ranking according to position.[17] I was provided with a chair, which I took with me as I progressed from one end of the office to the other.

Though not a native speaker, my fluency in written and spoken Sinhala was perhaps the most vital tool in my bag of skills as a researcher. Sinhala is the official language, and all transactions, oral and written, are conducted in that language. In addition, while all but two members of the upper echelons of the administration were bilingual, the rest of the clerks and all the grama sevakas and minor employees spoke Sinhala exclusively. It cannot be emphasized enough that my ability to communicate in Sinhala "like a native," as they frequently put it, helped me to establish rapport with the officials and their clients, and also made me aware of the subtle nuances of written and spoken Sinhala.

As the weeks progressed, I was invited to join in the tea and lunch breaks. Very often at the end of the day I would walk back to my home in the company of those officials whose bus stops lay in that direction, or with others who accompanied us on their bicycles. On occasion the AGA would give me a ride in his car. These were occasions for informal interviews and a valuable source of information which was inaccessible during work hours due to the pressing demands of office routine. I also had the opportunity to interview the AGA in his home.

Let me return to the question of whether my being a woman, more specifically a local, and at the time a single woman, influenced the research. With the five females in the office of the AGA, all of whom were approximately my age, I developed a easy camaradarie. With the four older and two younger males, my interactions were easy and informal. My relationship as a researcher with the three males of about my own age was marked by the culturally defined friendly restraint characteristic of interaction between members of the opposite sex of the same age. The latter would ooccasionally go out for a cigarette or a drink, and I was not asked to join them. Aside from the fact that I neither smoked nor drank, facts which they may or may not have known, the cultural impropriety of it would have inhibited them from issuing such an invitation. For the same reason I would not have gone with them.

Field visits or "circuits" in the company of the AGA were another source of information. In colonial times and immediately afterwards, a field visit to the site of a problem was the task of the GA. It might be to look at land under dispute, or to draw boundaries for land allotments. Today this task falls upon the AGA, and I participated in three circuits. They were occasions to observe interaction between the AGA and his clients, away from the office and on the client's turf. The notable feature of the circuits was the lack of formality; decisions made on circuit are subsequently formalized by the client through a visit to the office.

The observer-client aspect of the study remains to be addressed. Very often, cases came in rapid succession and the task of keeping up with a notebook and pen seemed impossible. Very soon, however, I observed a pattern. Clients gathered outside the office at opening time and rushed to get the attention of the officials upon their arrival. But there was nearly always a lull in the afternoon, and I took this opportunity to complete writing up the events that I had been unable to commit to paper in the morning. Since the emphasis of the study was on official-client interaction, I spent the major part of my time observing actual transactions. Occasionally, I was able to obtain further information from a client upon his

return to the community or through others within my face-to-face
network. At no time did I encounter a reluctance to talk,
either on the part of the official or the clients. As the
research progressed, officials would often volunteer
information, stating, "this would be an interesting thing to be
included in your book," and I have indeed included much of that
in my dissertation and in this book.

Historical and background material was collected in two
stages. While conducting field observations, I used the
kachcheri archives. I also collected a life history and a
series of interviews from a former GA who has had an illustrious
career as an administrator. His insights as an administrator,
tempered by the eye of a social scientist, enriched the archival
description of late colonial times continuing through the
mid-1960s. During the elections (of 1976-77), when routine
administration was at a standstill and the resources and
manpower of the kachcheri were geared to preparing for the poll,
I spent about two months working in the files of the Department
of National Archives in Colombo.

To summarize, a command of Sinhala (the official language,
and the language spoken by approximately 90 percent of the
population in that area), together with a fluency in Tamil (the
language of most of the rest),[18] enabled me to understand not
only the spoken word, but also its nuances. This skill was
crucial. Second, as a citizen of the same nation and having
grown up within the larger Sinhalese-Buddhist culture (although
I was not a part of it), I knew how to establish rapport with
"my" people. That status of virtual insider helped rather than
hindered the process of recognizing implicit meaning, which has
to be made explicit for cultural analysis, as Obeyesekere
insists (1981:11): "I am one with them and yet not one of
them."

With gratitude and affection, I have acknowledged the
willingness with which officials welcomed me into their domain
and the readiness with which they shared written and oral

information, fully aware of the very visible presence of my notebook and pen. Likewise, I am grateful to the clients who bared their problems in my presence. They had my assurance of anonymity and in recognition of this trust, I have changed or withheld the names of individuals, as well as the location.

FOOTNOTES

1. Ceylon was renamed Sri Lanka in 1972. In this work, the older name will be retained in references dealing with instances prior to that time.

2. At the time this research was conducted, there were 22 administrative districts. This number was later increased to 24.

3. Regional differences are identified as low-country, or the coastal plains, and up-country, or the central hills. Culturally, this distinction is relevant for the Sinhalese inhabitants, who are distinguished as Low-Country Sinhalese and Up-Country Sinhalese, respectively.

4. To Geertz (1973:311-26) I owe the inspiration for this line of thinking in my research.

5. This position is derived from Max Weber's insistence that human beings are "cultural beings endowed with the capacity and the will to take a deliberate attitude towards the world and lend it significance," (1948:81). An individual is not passive, according to Weber's notion of culture, but uses and manipulates cultural meaning (cf. Obeyesekere 1981:10).

6. Food shortage due to flood or drought is an example of the first, while the creation of the DPA is an instance of the second.

7. It must be noted that the minor employees formerly known as peons do not have their own seats.

8. For a discussion of this position, see Obeyesekere (Ibid., p. 18).

9. This distinction follows Firth (1951:35-36), who states "the more one thinks of (social) structure of a society in abstract terms of group relations or of ideal patterns, the more necessary it is to think separately of social organization in terms of concrete activity."

10. The following instance comes to mind: Like others of her colleagues at different times, clerk Kamala tells a client "Why this great hurry? If you rush me you will never get this done."

11. Max Weber (1973:95) makes a distinction between the politician and the administrator by saying that while the former

fights, the latter does not. The administrator in this case did precisely what Weber did not expect him to do, i.e., fight.

12.   Changes in personnel occurred through promotion and transfer. As a result, three individuals occupied the position of DRO/AGA at varying times. This was also the case for the positions of GA and Additional GA.

13.   While in most cases an area under the administration of a grama sevaka may be correctly designated as a village, given the urban-rural mix of the population, in some cases these regions are wholly, if not largely, urban.

14.   According to 1972 census figures, at this time the administrative district had a population of 588,254 of which 66,357 were defined as urban. Of this the Ganvälla DRO/AGA division had a total of 156,403, of whom 36,641 were categorized as urban. In contrast, the second most populous division had a total population of 146,594 with an urban population of 16,480.

15.   Officials within the upper echelons of the administration were aware that this "book" was in fact a doctoral dissertation.

16.   Officials are transferable and often posted out of their hometowns. While this was true of the GA and his aides, it was less true of those in the office of the DRO/AGA. Here, one official had occupied the same position for 10 years and all three AGAs were members of the local community.

17.   Formally, the administrative hierarchy is three-tiered. The AGA is a member of the Sri Lanka Administrative Service, and below him are the clerks who are members of the Sri Lanka Clerical Service. The minor employees occupy the bottom of the office hierarchy. The grama sevakas have their own offices in their division, pay frequent visits to the office of the AGA, and belong to a separate Grama Sevaka Service.

18.   English-speaking Burghers, descendants of Portuguese and Dutch settlers, comprise approximately one percent of the population.

CHAPTER 2

The Bureaucratic Persona:

the Indigenous System, the Colonial Period,

and the Present

Patrimonial Administration[1]

The system of regional and central administration that
existed in Ceylon before Portuguese conquest of the-low country
districts in 1505 was patrimonial (Weber 1978:1006-38).
Landlord and tenant were the principal actors. Land ownership
was the basis of power and position in society and the
administrative system was a model of the social system.

The _dissava_ was the regional head of the patrimonial
bureaucracy, and his administrative province was the _dissavany_.
He was chosen by the king from among those of the appropriate
caste who had the ruler's confidence. The _dissava_ held office
for a year (though his tenure could be extended at the king's
pleasure) and he paid an annual _däkum_ [dues] into the king's
treasury. Upon appointing the _dissava_, the king presented him
with a horse or an elephant, both considered royal animals.
This action validated the appointment.

Within his province, the _dissava_ possessed both judicial and
executive authority. He "owned" all land in the _dissavany_ and
commanded the services of his tenants in return for the use of
this land (Pieris 1956:23). He was a man of consequence
(Dewaraja 1972:179); he rode a palanquin within his district,
and upon his arrival or departure, a salute of _kodituwakku_
[gingalls, or heavy muskets] was fired. Banners called _maha_
kodi and _del_ _kodi_ were also part of the paraphernalia of his
office.

Each _dissava_ had his own administrative staff, which he
personally selected from among the _ratē_ _attho_ [local

aristocracy]. Their appointments also depended on their caste
rank and on the dissava's pleasure. In recognition of this
privilege, he received from each appointee a bulat surulla:
forty leaves of betel on which were placed coins, the number
being determined by custom. Since appointments were given to
the highest bidder, the dissava might in fact receive more than
was customary. In addition, certain castes paid mura ridi, a
fee in commutation of service. Finally, all fines levied in the
course of administering justice went into the dissava's
treasury.

The dissava's tenants were his clients. In return for the
privilege of being allowed to settle on his land, they performed
rajakariya [services] for the dissava according to their caste
positions, made dakum offerings during the New Year and on
ceremonial occasions, and behaved obsequiously in his presence.

In summary, the patrimonial administration of the dissavany
had the following characteristics. Appointments to office were
based on hereditary status (that is, on caste) and were a
privilege rather than a right; they depended upon the good will
of the bestower. For the clients, the use of the dissava's land
was also a privilege rather than a right. It, too, depended on
the good will of the dissava. In both cases, the maintenance of
good will was ensured by paying dues and displaying an
obsequious demeanor. There was no fixed salary attached to the
office, no separation of office from home, and no distinction
between official and private sources of income. The powers and
privileges of office were appropriated (Weber 1978:44) by the
official as his own. Ceremonial behavior attached to the
office, and the rigidly hierarchical nature of society in
general and of the administration in particular, produced a
formalism which distanced the official from his client. Such
formalism, however, did not isolate the official. The
successful official was the one who allowed the appropriate
clients -- on the appropriate occasions -- to penetrate the
official persona and gain access to him.

Administration Under the Portuguese and Dutch

When the Portuguese conquered the low-country districts of
Ceylon in 1505, they retained this patrimonial administrative
system as their model (Abeyasinghe 1966:91; de Silva 1972:12).
But they did not understand the nuances of the system, and the
district officials gained considerable autonomy. At the best
of times, given the poor communications between the center and
the province, the dissava had considerable power; under the
Portuguese this was further enhanced.

The dissavas and their subordinates were almost always
selected from among the allies of the Portuguese and not
necessarily always from the traditional ruling elite. Officials
appointed in such a manner increased the coercive, autocratic
nature of the administration and diminished its paternalism.
There was a greater distance between the ruler and the ruled.
Formalism now went hand in hand with impersonal relations and
uncaring, relatively unconstrained authorities. This trend
continued during the period of Dutch East India Company rule in
Ceylon, which lasted from 1658 to 1798 (Arasaratnam 1958:120;
Colin R. de Silva 1953:9; Goonewardene 1958:148-49).

By the end of the Dutch period, the office of the dissava
had become exclusively Dutch. The Dutch also began to pay
accomodessans [salaries] to officials, in order to reduce the
size of the land grants they received. The salaries were low,
and varied according to a person's rank and office. While the
higher officials fared better in terms of the size of their
supplementary land grants, the headmen of lower grade received
greatly reduced, uniformly fixed portions of land determined by
their ranks. As a result, these petty officials intensified
their control over their tenant-inhabitants.

During the centuries of Portuguese and Dutch domination, the
administrative system of maritime Ceylon changed from a
traditional, formal, personal one dependent upon ceremony and
based on reciprocal obligations determined by caste, service

tenure, and ties to the land. It became instead a system of
formalism which lacked the personal and paternalistic concern of
the administrator toward his subjects. Relationships were
increasingly non-reciprocal, and the sense of awe associated
with the person in office (Abeyasinghe 1966:75) increasingly
became one of fear.

Many officials in the provincial administration of Ceylon's
maritime districts were outsiders when the British arrived.
Assigned to areas over which they had authority, where they
owned and controlled land, they derived their power from the
foreign authority, under whose shadow they exploited the
subjects who came under their control. In the words of
Additional Government Agent Wimalasiri,

> There was a great degree of impersonality in
> the system [of administration] in the times of
> the British as compared to the up-country
> [Kandyan] areas. In the low country, unlike
> in the Kandyan areas, the dissavas and
> mudaliyars were appointed by the Portuguese
> and the Dutch and they were often mere clerks
> for Colombo who exploited the people. This
> memory lingers on (field notes, 1976).

The Origin and Development
of Civil Service Bureaucracy

Regional administration underwent profound change under
British rule, which began in 1798. The British East India
Company abolished the patrimonial system of administration and
replaced it with South Indian officials. Administration was by
districts, then called kachcheri,[2] a name which has continued
to the present. There were rigorous protests and the old
system, with some modification, was brought back with British
officials at the top of the hierarchy (Collins 1951:14; Tennant
1859:74). From that time onwards, the policy of the colonial

government was to maintain the administrative status quo, making modifications only when necessary and expedient.

A type of civil service was introduced to Ceylon in 1798 (Toussaint 1933:1-2). It was based on patronage, and the social connections of the candidates were a major consideration: a young man from a socially or politically prestigious family could be sure of receiving an appointment. Together with patronage went a belief that administrative authority could be entrusted only to those whose social status was such that its exercise would be instinctive. This criterion for selection was continued into the middle ranks (comprising natives of Dutch descent) and into the lower ranks (Sinhalese and Tamil mudaliyars and headman).

The low-country districts of Ceylon were divided into six collectorates (Colombo, Jaffna, Matara, Trincomalee, Batticoloa and Puttalam), each under a collector. Generally a senior civil servant, he was sometimes assisted by a junior, and by the kachcheri mudaliyar, some European clerks, and various inferior native officials. This establishment was called the kachcheri. The functions of the collector were laid down in Maitland's Minute of 1808. It stated that every collector should move among the people, traveling extensively in his province so as to know the conditions in which they lived:

> The first general object for every collector
> is to make himself acquainted with the various
> districts in his province and the various
> headmen belonging to such districts by making
> frequent circuits through the whole province..
> ..It must be necessary here to add that in all
> instances, and on every occasion the greatest
> moderation be displayed to the whole of the
> natives by the Collectors....That the power
> delegated by the government to the Collector
> be made use of with consideration and

> forbearance and that they consider the only
> mode of ensuring the respect and conciliating
> the feelings of the natives to be, by
> adopting a line of conduct at once firm, but
> moderate and considerate (Kannangara 1966:65).

Under Governor Maitland, the administrative service became a
career with adequate remuneration and pensions for officials.

Over the next 100 years, the colonial civil service
underwent a gradual change. The collector was replaced by the
government agent (GA). Official minutes at various times
determined positions, hierarchy, salaries, pensions, and
requirements for entry into the service.[3]

The British civil servants came mainly from the upper
classes and had been educated in public schools. The qualities
of a good public servant, said to be acquired at public school
(and later at Oxford or Cambridge), were courage, adaptability,
firmness, enterprise, and sympathy. These were the qualities of
"gentlemen," and the official was expected to display them in
all circumstances.[4] Huessler (1963:82-106) says that the
public school implanted the ethos of service. The colonial
officials were not merely civil servants with a duty to govern,
but were also responsible for protecting and guiding native
people. The public school was reckoned to be adult life in
microcosm: benevolent, and not egalitarian. Such training was
essential before one could become a ruler. Part of this
indoctrination was the "benevolent dictatorship of the prefect
system."[5] Prefects were selected by the school authorities
rather than elected. They were supposed to rule by force of
example rather than by coercion.

There were also family influences on the colonial civil
servant: the austere impersonal relationships of the English
upper class. Remote parents and transitory nannies forced the
child to look for outside sources (the school, in this case) of
affection and support. The resulting relationship between the
leader (master) and followers (boys) is regarded by Huessler as

another crucial influence in the formation of the ethos of the colonial administrator. Furthermore, the social aloofness and reluctance to mingle with the crowd inculcated in the public schoolboy, coming as he did from a privileged class and belonging to a privileged institution, encouraged an authoritarian character in the colonial civil servant. According to Huessler (1963:92), "The same aloofness was continued in their experience with the subject people. Officials found natives worthy of one kind of treatment and the native aristocrats worthy of another." The English civil servants formed a homogeneous class of exclusive cultural background. Membership was rarely and reluctantly given to outsiders, and if a member "went native" he was despised.[6]

This self-image of the colonial civil servant fitted conveniently into the patrimonial administrative system, which was similarly authoritarian. Thus, Leonard Woolf states:

...quite apart from the complicated engine of
the imperial government Kandyan society was
purely feudal (traditional). The Nugawelas,
Ratwattes and all the other great Kandyan
land-owning families were feudal chiefs, and
the procession and tom toms and prostrations
which greeted the OA [Office Assistant in the
Kachcheri] were mere examples of manners
ordinarily displayed by the villagers to the
feudal chief, and now displayed towards the
highly sophisticated product of St. Paul's
School and Trinity College, Cambridge.
Moreover, I was up above in the feudal
hierarchy, one of the super chiefs,...and
however much one may dislike the fuss and
ceremony of social systems -- and I do hate
them -- one cannot be impervious to the
flattery of being a top dog liked by the under
dog. I certainly, all through my time in

> Ceylon, enjoyed my position and the flattery
> of being the great man and the father of the
> people (1967:157-58).

The members of this elite group of British civil servants
found the native traditional social environment and its
responses to authority quite compatible with their own outlook.
Nevertheless, the situation was strange. Behind the cloak of
authoritarian public school behavior, enhanced by traditional
Ceylonese ceremony, the British civil servants were bound by the
Rule of Law and by the traditions of the service. The latter
were derived from a mixture of platonic idealism and the
utilitarian and liberal humanitarian ideals of
nineteenth-century Britain, somewhat modified by eastern
experience. "Good government, economic improvement under the
Rule of Law, these ideals soon became the mission, the white
man's burden for the British bureaucracy" (Saparamadu
1959:xiii). This training did not allow for sympathy with local
values. The only concern was with good government as the
service knew it.

Senior Ceylonese administrators found themselves formally in
tune with the ethos of the colonial civil service. For the
native, English education and a leaning towards an English way
of life were essential prerequisites for appointment. Such an
education was the privilege of an exclusive group whose members
could afford to send their sons to exclusive private schools in
Ceylon and the to prestigious British universities.[7] Thus the
early Ceylonese civil servants were members of the upper and
upper middle classes -- the traditional landed aristocracy and
later, the planting interest. Coming from a background of the
traditional ruling class, and by virtue of the education
available to them (Fernando 1970:74), they easily identified
with the ethos of the authoritarian colonial civil service. The
sons and grandsons of the traditional chiefs were among the

earliest Ceylonese civil servants, and they continued to exercise this new authority in much the same way their ancestors had under the old system.

In short, the bureaucratic persona found in the Ceylon civil service at the height of British colonial rule was a curious mixture of platonic idealism, paternalistic British liberalism, and Ceylonese traditionalism. These characteristics shared an orientation towards an exclusive, hierarchical administrative system: a hierarchy of class for the British and of caste and class for the Ceylonese.

The GA was usually a senior civil servant and was referred to as the disāpati hāmuduruvō; the first term was the name for the dissava under the traditional administration, while the second meant "lord" in Sinhala. His dwelling, called the "residency," was equal in importance to the homes (valavvas) of the dissavas. Finally, the "circuits" which the GA made in his division had a ceremonial flavor reminiscent of tours by officials under the old system.[8] As was the case with the other civil servants at the time, the GAs were subject to the control of the secretary of state and the governor in matters of appointments, promotions, transfers, and discipline. Within these controls, subject to the Rule of Law and to their own internalized values of "service as duty," the GAs were masters of their domains. Slow communication between Colombo (the locus of central authority) and the provinces frequently left real power in the hands of the provincial ruler. The duties and authority of the GA were considerable. He was the chief representative of the government in his area and was vested with all the executive authority of the state in his domain. GAs were also revenue officers, charged with seeing to it that all revenue due to the government was collected and that payments from the government were disbursed. Through a system of petitions, the GA ensured that these tasks were adequately carried out by his subordinates.[9] In addition, he was responsible for implementing the law and doing the work of other

state departments which did not have local organizations of
their own.

The native headmen of various ranks provided the link
between the civil servant and the citizen. Nevertheless, in the
eyes of the colonial government, there was a clear distinction
between the native official and the civil servant. At no time
was it envisaged that the former would evolve into the latter
(Kannangara 1974:83; Administrative Report 1870:142).

Administrative reforms undertaken in 1931 and 1944
(Warnapala 1974) were intended to ensure the impartiality of the
civil service in matters of appointments, discipline, and the
dismissal of officials. These changes brought the formal
structure of the civil service closer to the Weberian ideal type
of rational organization (1978:956-63) than at any time before
or since. At this time there were also changes affecting the
lower echelons. In 1935, the chief headmen were replaced by a
class of civil service officials known as divisional revenue
officers or DRO, recruited not on the basis of family
connections as in the case of the headmen, but through
competitive examinations. In 1948 Ceylon became an independent
nation-state, but further administrative reform had to wait
until 1962, when the village headmanship was abolished, and
replaced by the grama sevaka service. Officials at the village
level were now recruited on the basis of uniform educational
qualifications and competitive examinations, and became subject
to transfer. At the same time, the civil service was abolished;
it was replaced by the Ceylon (later Sri Lanka) Administrative
Service (CAS or SLAS). The main feature of the new service was
the unified administrative class. A uniform method of
recruitment was introduced: all officers would have equal
opportunity for entry into the higher ranks of the service.
Technical officers who had hitherto functioned separately were
now included in the unified class.

More important than these structural changes was a
transformation in the bureaucratic persona. At every stage in

its evolution, this persona has been the product of interaction between official and client. In the eyes of the official, this persona is self symbolized in a social position, prestige and esteem, finding validation within its culture. Under the patrimonial administration with its linked features of formalism and personalism, social ties merged with administrative ties. Under the Portuguese and the Dutch, there was a change: appointments were confined to their native allies and to Ceylonese of European descent, the Burghers. In British times, appointments were limited to the traditional elite who were their allies and to the traveled, English-educated Ceylonese middle class which shared with the ruler-administrator a common cultural heritage secured through an English education. Since independence, and especially since 1956, there has been greater participation of the masses in the political process. This is attributable to the rise of the Sinhala-educated rural intelligensia, itself a product of a system of free education begun in 1941. Thus, there has been a demand for access to officials from a hitherto excluded group, and this has, in fact, turned out to be a demand for personalism. But, given the difference in values between the administrator and the Sinhala-educated rural intelligensia, this demand has been difficult if not impossible to meet. The post-1956 critique of the bureaucracy as unfeeling (and therefore ineffective), the subsequent attempts by popular political figures to decentralize the administration and "take it to the people," the increasing influence of elected represenatives like the MP in determining policy and making decisions, and the creation of such instruments of formal political power as the political authority to control and supervise the bureaucracy, can all be attributed to this demand for personal contact. On the other hand, as opportunities for the son of the rural peasant to become an administrator increased, channels for mediation between the masses and the administrators became available.

Positions of responsibility and authority in the traditional system of administration were associated with much prestige, power, and formalism. This was also the case under the Portuguese, the Dutch, and subsequently the British. This continues today even though positions in the public service are no longer the only source of power and prestige, as they had been under colonial rule. Officials complain frequently about their inadequate salaries, saying that what makes it still worthwhile to be an administrator is the prestige accompanyng their positions. It is important to note that for the liberal arts educated, this remains the only direct access to a power-prestige position. Studying for a law degree and/or joining the political arena are the other alternatives, but these require financial resources and a special type of outlook which may not be found in the average citizen with a liberal arts education. This situation is further enhanced by the fact that the majority of the liberal arts educated are also the product of free education. The peasant's dream was to educate his son to become an ējanta [government agent].

But, as this becomes a reality, the bureaucratic persona projected by the official from a rural-peasant background is not radically different from that of his predecessors. Taking them as his reference group, he exercises the powers of his position in much the same style as his counterpart from the days of patrimonial and colonial administration. Against this, his clients demand more of the "personal touch" in official-client interaction. As will be shown, the successful administrator is the one who finds the right balance between the formal and the personal, all within the framework of an administration formally corresponding to the Weberian model of rational authority.

The evolution of the bureaucratic persona from the patrimonial to the colonial and beyond, has left a significant impact on the contemporary form and function of the bureaucracy. The formal structure of the kachcheri administration is a legacy of British rule. The actual

behavioral themes found with it reflect the cultural values of
the people (both officials and clients); these values are
synthesized from indigenous social values, the traditional
patrimonial system, and values introduced by the British.
"Formalistic impersonality" (Weber 1964:340) is the essence of
the ideal type of bureaucratic persona. History and culture
have determined the specific nature of this persona in Sri Lanka
today.

FOOTNOTES

1. This description of the patrimonial system of
administration in Ceylon is based on studies by Pieris (1956),
Hettiarachy (1972), and Dewaraja (1972).

2. This Tamil name was given by the aumildars [South Indian
officials] to the office of the revenue collector, which
subsequently became the office of the GA.

3. The Colebrooke-Cameron Reforms were considered a major
landmark in this direction (see Mendis: 1956:xi-xii).

4. Leonard Woolf (1967:36) considers being a "good fellow
or good gentleman" as crucial for appointment to high places.
Woolf, the husband of author Virginia Woolf, was Assistant
Government Agent in the Hambantota district in the low country
of Ceylon from 1908 to 1911. His Diaries in Ceylon and Growing
-- an Autobiography still rank among the most illuminating
accounts of the experiences of a colonial administrator in
Ceylon.

5. According to Huessler, the closest American equivalent
to prefects are members of the student council.

6. LeMesurier, a civil servant who became a convert to
Islam in order to marry a second wife, was dismissed from the
service even though he was within the law.

7. According to Warnapala (1974:65), graduates of Oxford,
Cambridge, Edinburgh, London, Dublin, and Manchester
Universities monopolized the Ceylon Civil Service.

8. To quote a former GA:
   One could say that in the early days, i.e., in
   the forties, the circuit was quite similar to
   the Mahanaduva (the King's court of justice).
   The GA rode a horse. One of the requirements
   of the Ceylon Civil Service examination was to
   pass a horseback riding test, and one was
   given a horse allowance. The horse was not
   any old animal. It was the king's animal,
   which had also been used by the conquering
   Portuguese and Dutch generals. No lesser
   official could ride a horse. It gave a real
   sense of power. You were high up away from
   the lesser mortals. You could from up there
   talk down to a man [a client]. To me it was
   literally to ride a high horse....This field
   visit was a major event. Plans were made well
   in advance, there was a predetermined route,
   circuit bungalows were set up to serve as

resting places, you were accompanied by other
officials like peons [minor employees] and
interpreters. There was a pre-announcement
that the GA was coming. This enabled the
people to come and present their grievances in
open public court."

9. A GA's administrative report states, "En passant I may
remark that though the 'right of petition' is considered
elsewhere the safeguard of the subject, in Ceylon it is
undoubtably the greatest protection the government and its
servants possess, keeping them informed of all current events
and the actions of their subordinate officers: 'giving
petitions' being equivalent to the British practice of writing
to the local paper -- a petition to the Governor ranking with a
'letter to the Times'."

CHAPTER 3
Personalization and Accessibility

A bureaucracy formally based on rational norms, imposed upon a sociocultural environment in which such norms are alien, resulted in the dual nature of public administration in Sri Lanka. On the one hand there is a formal commitment to and acceptance of the rationalized structure of administration. On the other hand -- at the behavioral level, in interacting face-to-face -- officials and clients introduce the norms and values of their cultures (Anderson 1972). These are in opposition to the norms and values of the formal structure of the bureaucracy. Similar nonbureaucratic values also appear in the interaction of officials with one another.

Formal Structure of the Administration
and the Normative Position of the Official

An official's normative position is defined in Weber's "ideal type" of legitimate domination[1] as legal authority with a bureaucratic administrative staff. Such bureaucracies, according to Weber, are rationally established for reasons of expediency, through agreement or by imposition. They claim obedience from the members of the society.

The Ceylon Public Service, which evolved into the Sri Lanka Public Service, was created by British colonial rulers building on an existing administrative framework, in order to maintain tranquility and serve British mercantile interests. This was achieved through a series of constitutional reforms enforced by the British Colonial Office, the governor of Ceylon, and the local legislature, and became binding law on the citizens of Ceylon.

Further, according to Weber (1969b:330-31), authority and
functions of bureaucracies are defined by rules, an office is
organized on the principle of hierarchy with a right of appeal
from the lower to the higher official, and the selection of
candidates is based on merit. The office constitutes a career
for the official and there is a system of promotion according to
seniority, or achievement, or both. Officials are paid
stipulated salaries in cash with a right to a pension and they
are subject to strict and systematic discipline and control in
the conduct of the office. The homes of the administrative
staff are separated from their place of work. Finally,
administrative acts, decisions and rules are recorded in
writing.

In its office organization, recruitment of personnel, and
allocation of functions, the Sri Lanka Public Service
approximates these criteria and therefore formally qualifies as
a modern bureaucracy in the Weberian sense. All welfare or
development functions initiated and carried out by the national
government in any part of the country are entrusted to this
bureaucracy. The public service is staffed by four general
service categories -- the administrative service, the clerical
service, the grama sevakas, and the minor employees. At the
provincial level, each kachcheri is staffed by officials from
these four categories.

In order to qualify for entry into these services,
applicants must have a minimum education: for example, a
bachelors degree for the administrative service or a high school
education for the clerical and grama sevaka services.
Candidates for all three services must sit for a written
competitive examination, and those who are selected on the basis
of their performance in this exam are subject to an oral
examination. Applicants are chosen on the basis of their
performance in both. Appointments, promotions, discipline,
transfer, and overall supervision of the personnel in the
administrative services were originally in the hands of the

public service commission (as provided for under the Soulbury
Constitution), and later under the state service administrative
board and the state services disciplinary board, under the
Republic Constitution of Sri Lanka.[2] This was done in order
to ensure administrative impartiality and to guarantee the
independence of the bureaucracy.[3] It is said that these
structures routinize the work of the public servant, who "has
become a cog in the huge wheel of the Administration"
(Anonymous 1953:44-45). In fact, as we shall see, there are
other forces which also influence behavior.

Varying Expectations

In recent years this rigid, impersonal facade of the public
service has been the subject of much criticism. Thus, it is
said that,

> ...protected and guarded by barriers, boards,
> attendants and designations, the Public
> Servant can make an ivory tower of his office.
> The minutes he makes in his files, the
> standardized forms he uses, the stereotyped
> style of correspondence, the formalized
> officialese, the hackneyed procedures tend to
> make his work impersonal and frigid. This
> highly institutionalized and rigidly
> formalistic approach to 'public service'
> ironically makes the public servant
> inaccessible to the public (Ibid.).

With the increasing role of the state in national development,
"the demands made on the public servant have changed
radically...the neutral, impartial, impersonal public servant as
conceived earlier is as negative in character as the rules,
regulations and red tape within which he works" (Ibid.).

On a similar note, the Report of the Public Service
Commission says that:

...what is needed now and always is drive and
initiative at the top; mere ability to keep
the administrative machinery going is in
itself insufficient qualification for
promotion to posts of greater responsibility.
An efficient Government Service can only
result from a system which places a premium on
positive merit and disregards posts of
responsibility for officers whose careers
though without a blot or stain are clearly
colorless (1954:17).

Thus the Sri Lanka Public Service has formally emerged as an
approximation of the Weberian model -- "as a public service
above society, holding the scales with God-like indifference"
(Anonymous 1953:43-44). But, despite this framework, the
powers-that-be have had formal expectations of the members of
the service that have proven paradoxical. On the one hand, they
look for an administrator who identifies himself with his
official role to such an extent that he qualifies as a
"bureaucratic personality";[4] on the other hand, they expect an
administrator to have character and personality and to be
capable of taking the initiative, i.e., someone with charisma.
According to Samaraweera, "there is no doubt that 'red-tapism'
and centralized control continue to inhibit the bureaucracy,
preventing it from innovating and dealing in a flexible manner
with the public" (1974:32). This is especially true of the
lower and middle echelons of the administrative hierarchy. Thus
Divisional AGA Somapala frequently complained that all he did
was countersign documents, thereby becoming a "useless rubber
stamp." He professed to be "fed up" with this kind of work: "I
prefer work where one can use one's initiative, for example,
work associated with rural development. But, instead, most of
my time is taken up by signing permits or countersigning
certificates which, though they are essential statutory
functions, is boring routine."

At the higher levels, it is possible for officials to avoid
the "boring routine." But at the divisional level of
administration, further obstacles are placed in the way of the
official's initiative and decision-making capacity. This takes
the form of external political pressure exerted by the local
members of Parliament, backed by their networks of manipulatory
political power, reaching to the center of national politics and
culminating in the formalized institution of the political
authority. These pressures, while acting to stifle the
initiative and charisma of the official, paradoxically lead to
the emergence of a different type of charismatic official, that
is, one who successfully uses political strategies to survive
this pressure.

There is also a third and equally important constraint,
arising not from any formalized specific institutional source,
but from the diffused yet persistent influences of the
sociocultural environment within which the bureaucracy
operates. In Sri Lanka, legal authority via bureaucratic
administration is not the natural outgrowth of a highly
modernized, large-scale society as in the west; instead, it is
an imposition through legislation, from an outside source, onto
a society which even now is primarily small-scale and dependent
on face-to-face primary relationships.[5] These relationships
are based on ethnicity, caste, kinship, and other such
criteria. The Sri Lanka Public Service formally incorporates
most of the elements of the Weberian model. But, since it was
an administrative system which emerged from a semi-feudal
traditional environment and which was set in motion by a ruler
whose main goal was to leave that environment as undisturbed as
possible, it lacks a fundamental element crucial to the Weberian
ideal type of bureaucratic authority: the formal and impersonal
nature of official interactions.

Power, Status and Prestige:
The Self and Its Cultural Environment

According to Weber,

> ...the typical person in authority...in the
> actions associated with his status and the
> commands he issues to others is subject to an
> impersonal order to which his actions are
> oriented....The members of the corporate
> group, insofar as they obey a person in
> authority do not owe this obedience to him as
> an individual, but to the impersonal order.
> There is an obligation to obedience only
> within the sphere of the rationally delimited
> authority which, in terms of the order, has
> been conferred upon him (1969:330).

Since its inception, the Sri Lanka Public Service has been
characterized not by such an "impersonal order" but by a
personalistic orientation. Unlike the "formalistic
impersonalism" of the bureaucracy as it is enunciated in acts
and other documents, the personalistic orientation of the
officials and their clients is the result of a carry-over of a
value that is dominant in the social environment. This
particularistic[6] orientation of actions in a situation where
universalism[7] should be the norm is perhaps crucial to the
understanding of the dilemma facing the bureaucracy in Sri
Lanka.

In Samaraweera's words, "...the bureaucrat in Sri Lanka was
always a highly visible figure; he never functioned in cold
anonymity. The role he was required to play...not only by the
very nature of the structure of the administration but perhaps
even by the people whom he was ruling, was that of a 'benevolent
despot'" (1974:33). Similarly, an editorial in the journal
"Community" (1953) states, "Against the semi-feudal background
of public life in Ceylon some people having feudal notions may

think that the occupation of an office is comparable to the possession of a fief."

One may add to these sentiments the following proposition. In ego's official capacity, it is his personal self that is brought into play. An individual in his official capacity, irrespective of his relative position in the hierarchy, has tatvaya [status] and nambuva [prestige]. To maintain his status, ego must behave as is expected of him -- that is, he must wear the mask of formalism[8] -- lest he fall into a situation of 'no prestige' (tatvayaknā).

In the words of a former GA,

> ...even persons who don't have power, for
> example, peons, maintain this facade of having
> power. There is this official stance that one
> must not be too accessible -- then anybody can
> go to one. Other officials would tell me that
> I should not be too accessible, that a GA
> should not be seen by the ordinary people and
> that by being easily accessible I was letting
> the side down.

The power an official holds, however little it may be objectively, is magnified in the official's own estimation, and this is conveyed in his interactions with others. There is even an inverse relationship between the amount of actual power one holds and the extent of exaggeration of one's self-importance. Thus, interactions are oriented in terms of formalistic personalism rather than formalistic impersonality. In order to avoid falling into a situation of "no-prestige," the official takes the stance of maintaining prestige by not being too accessible.

There is also a move on the part of those who have a particular status, not merely to retain it but also to prevent others who are considered as not belonging to this particular status, from gaining entry into it. Thus, of all the "services" within the nation's public service, the Sri Lanka Administrative

Service (formerly the Ceylon Civil Service) has been the most
prestigious. There has been constant clamor by the "lower"
service to gain entry into the "higher" service. It has
repeatedly been alleged by the other services that the snob
elite in the administrative service deliberately keep out the
rest. To overcome this situation, provision was made for
absorbing personnel from the lower echelons while maintaining
the principle of direct recruitment to the SLAS. But a division
remained between the direct recruits and the others, and the
former were accused of assuming an elitist posture against the
latter. Thus the Staff Assistant of the Ganvälla AGA's
office told a friend that,

> ...in order to move from the clerical to the
> administrative service we have to take the
> limited competitive [examination] and then an
> Efficiency Bar Exam. There are plenty of
> capable people in the clerical service who
> don't get an opportunity to exercise their
> talents. It is the SLAS officers who
> structure the requirements for entry and they
> try to keep out the clerical servants. For
> selection to Class I, for example, they keep
> changing the conditions from time to time and
> then they hand-pick the recruits.

This jealously safeguarded, caste-like attitude of the
higher services towards the lower is further exemplified by the
following case:

Case One. The monthly meeting between the AGA and his grama
sevakas is referred to as Division Day. This particular AGA's
division encompasses 36 GS divisions and therefore has 36 grama
sevakas. Due to the lack of special facilities, these meetings
are held in the AGA's office -- a sort of inner sanctum within
the office proper. The building itself is badly ventilated,
stuffy and gloomy. Two-thirds of the floor space is taken up by

the AGA's accoutrements of office: a desk and chair, a safe, and a bookshelf with dust-laden volumes of administrative enactments. There are also 10 chairs. A wooden bench that can seat about six persons is brought in especially for Division Day meetings. Even though all 36 GS are not present at a particular meeting, conditions within the room are, to say the least, crowded and uncomfortable in hot tropical weather.

After frequent complaints and apologies by the AGA -- to me, the clerks and the GS -- about this situation, he writes to the government agent (GA) and asks the latter's permission to use the conference hall of the Public Service Club. Located two blocks from the AGA's office, the hall is spacious enough to accommodate 37 people [including the AGA] in comfort. Though the club is primarily a place of recreation for members of the public service, during office hours it is also used for meetings of administrative committees in the kachcheri if a large enough room cannot be found on the premises.

The AGA receives a refusal from the GA, the reason being that the club hall is already booked for another meeting. The next month the AGA decides to book the place in advance, and receives in reply a notation at the bottom of his own letter of request; it merely says kanagatuyi [sorry], and is signed by the GA. A third attempt evokes the same response, and the AGA angrily announces to the GS that the club is not available.

Clerk Chandra subsequently volunteers the reason for the GA's terse refusal. According to her, it is because of an incident which occurred on the last occasion when the club was lent for a Division Day meeting: the GS had spat betel chew on the floor and on the white walls, leaving indelible stains.

Not only do the GA and his high-ranking officers generally belong hierarchically to an entirely different level than do the divisional AGA and (especially) the GS; they also come from different social backgrounds. The former are college-educated members of the English-Sinhala educated middle class, while the GS are from a village-peasant background and have no more than a

high school education. In the eyes of the former, the latter
are uncouth, ill-refined and outside of their class -- whether
administrative or social. The privilege of using the club was
withdrawn from them because they did not know how to use the
premises. However, this was not a valid reason for refusal, or
one that could be openly admitted to; hence the monosyllabic
refusal.

The official stance of not being too accessible -- the
bureaucratic persona -- is used by an officer to maintain his
personal prestige. There is also an expectation, at least on
the part of some clients, that officials will be fair and
effective because they limit accessibility. This is
illustrated by the following case.

Case Two. A middle-aged village woman makes a complaint to
the AGA about a property dispute. Her husband jointly owned a
property with 12 others; this gave them the right to four
coconut trees on the land. Since her husband's death, his
brothers have broken the fence [the land being fenced into 13
plots] and forcibly taken her trees.

The AGA tells the client that she should go back and make a
complaint to the GS of her division. The client replies that
the GS is a friend of the accused and had warned her not to
pluck coconuts from her own trees. Therefore, he is certain not
to give her a sympathetic hearing. This is why, she says, she
has come to the AGA's office to have her case heard by a
'respectable officer' (sāhena nilādnariyekuta kiyala vādē karavā
ganna). By this she means an official who maintains a distance
and is therefore not accessible to diverse influences in the
community. The implication is that the GS is not such an
officer.

As each official maintains his status and the higher ranks
maintain theirs vis-àa-vis the lower ranks, the latter try to

divest themselves of any "servile" connotations attached to their respective designations. Thus, the grama sevakas [servants of the village] demanded and were allowed to be called grama seva niladaris [rural service officers]. In fact, at one Division Day meeting, the GS complained that despite the change in title, letters still came to them from the AGA's office, using the old designation. They received the apologies of the AGA and his assurance that this practice would not be repeated. Upon hearing this, the GS also requested that the AGA supply them with name plates and an official seal with the new designation. Meanwhile, the clerical service union requested that the Minister of Public Administration change the name of their service, and this request was being considered by the minister. However, the grama sevakas and the clerks had been anticipated by the peons, who had succeeded in having themselves called karyala karya sahayaka [assistant in official duties].

In interactions with clients, there are some transactions which an official can legitimately do, and others which he pretends to be able to do. In the latter case, an official will go through his own networks of power within the office to complete a transaction for a client. If the transaction is successful then he (not the official who actually completes the task) claims the rewards -- actual or potential, material and non-material -- arising from the transaction. This is illustrated by the following case.

Case Three. A young male client walks towards the food control section of the AGA's office with a rice ration book in hand. On his way he recognizes clerk Chandra and stops by her desk to tell her that he needs to transfer his book from administrative region A to B. He adds, 'Can't I get this done today?' Simon, an office worker who has been listening to this conversation, tells the client, 'To do that you must have a letter from your GS vouching for your ownership of this book and then come back at the beginning of next week. Books are not transferred on the first week of the month' [which this particular week was]. Chandra adds that the letter from the GS is a must. The client replies that if he waits until next week, he will not be able to get this week's rations.

Upon hearing this, Chandra says to Simon, 'If I don't do this for him, he will not stop the bus for me. Now when he sees me, he stops the bus even if I am still walking towards the bus stop and even if there is only standing room on the footboard' [traveling on the footboard is illegal, and if detected the driver, the conductor and the traveler are all liable for fines]. Evidently the client is the driver of a bus which runs between Chandra's home town and the office. Simon tells the client, 'In that case you had better bring the letter from the GS because that will have the number of your householder's list[9] and then we will transfer your book immediately.'

As the client leaves, Chandra tells Simon that 'If I don't do a favor like this he will not stop the bus for me [meaning once the bus is full, which Chandra says is invariably the case by the time it reaches her stop]. Even yesterday he stopped the bus for me even though he did not admit any others.' Simon tells her that everything is settled now, that it will look even more impressive because he pretended to refuse while she obtained a concession from him for the client. Simon concludes that the client will be more obliged than ever to Chandra, since one must not do a favor easily, even if it is possible to do so -- favors must be made to appear difficult to obtain.

In this case, the client's personal contact is Chandra, but transferring rice ration books is not her job. It is up to clerk Rodrigo. Meanwhile, it is Simon's task to locate the correct Householder's List from among the bound volumes of such lists, and to lift it off the shelf and place it on Rodrigo's desk. Thus Simon and Rodrigo perform the transaction. However, since Chandra is seen to grant the favor to the client, she stands to benefit from the transaction.

Similarly, the failure of such a transaction results in shame and loss of face, as revealed in the following case.

Case Four. A middle-aged male client hands a letter to Chandra. It reads as follows: 'Dear daughter, the person who brings this is an older brother by relationship. I kindly request you to attend to his request with utmost care. Yours -- Uncle Davith.' The client has asked for a permit to transfer timber, and Chandra takes the letter over to Kamala, who handles this subject. Kamala reads the letter and says to Chandra, 'So he calls you daughter' [emphasizing the special nature of the transaction]. Chandra then tells Kamala that the letter is from a mama [mother's brother] of hers. Kamala checks her file and says that the particular permit is not written yet, adding as an afterthought, 'Even if I wrote it today, the AGA is not here to sign it.' The client overhears this and asks Chandra whether he should come back the following day. The staff assistant, who has listened to the conversation, tells the client that the AGA will not be back the next day, but that he will certainly return the day after. The client says, 'In that case I will have to make a change in the date of transport and make fresh arrangements.' As the client leaves, Chandra tells me that her mama had made this special request of her, and that he will now assume that she has no regard for his word: 'While it is true that the AGA is not here today, if only Kamala had done her job and had the permit ready yesterday, the AGA would have signed the permit before he left.' Chandra feels resentful toward Kamala for placing her in a situation where she, rather than Kamala, stands to lose face.

If favors are granted, they must be recognized as favors. Thus, if a particular official is approached by a client to negotiate a transaction, the latter should not also approach another official about the same problem. This is evident in the following instance.

Case Five. An old women who has come to see Chandra tells
me, 'I am from Chandra's village and I came to get some help
from her so that I can get my welfare money. I made out an
application some time back and I haven't heard anything since
then.' When Chandra arrives 10 minutes later, the client begins
to repeat her story. Chandra interrupts, saying, 'Give me a
minute to catch my breath and settle down.' She then says,
'Yes, I know that you brought me an application to be handed
over to Karunapala' [who handles the subject of social
welfare].' She checks with him, but he says that the
application is not on file. Chandra returns to the client and
says, 'Merely handing in an application is not enough; you must
come constantly and press your case. You did not come either to
my house or to the office and remind me. Now you better fill in
a fresh application.'

As Chandra walks back towards her desk, the client says to
her, 'Mawalage liyanamahattaya [a clerk named Mawalage] also
told me to come to you' [i.e., the clerk from the house of
Mawalage -- a kinship category]. At this, Chandra becomes
visibly annoyed and tells the client, 'Don't come and say to me
that he or anyone else need tell me to do a favor for a fellow
villager, someone I know.' The client becomes defensive and
says, 'Yes, I know, you are our child, no? (apē lamaya nē),' and
hurriedly leaves the office. Chandra then turns to me and says,
'I have had a lot of trouble from this liyanamahattaya. During
the last cement shortage I used to get an endless clientele who
would say that he had sent them to me. As if this were not
enough, he would himself bring clients and tell the AGA that
those requests were for persons known to me. He is very cunning
and is using me to gain his political ends; by claiming to
satisfy the clients' demands he gets their support for his
political party. I don't care about that, but I don't like him
exploiting me. Besides, even though he calls himself
liyanamahattaya he is not a clerk, he is a mere typist in the
courts.'

The client made a tactical error in mentioning that she was sent by another clerk. By doing so, she symbolically transferred some of the material and non-material benefits that might come out of the transaction to the liyanamahattaya, thereby divesting Chandra of what she felt was rightfully hers.

A transaction is a dyadic performance[10] between an official and a client. The entry of another official into this situation steals the limelight. This is not done. Here is an example.

Case Six. A client who is a coconut plucker in Chandra's village asks her to get him a new rice ration book to replace one that has lapsed. Since he lacks the customary letter of certification from the GS of his area, Chandra sends him back for it. Meanwhile, Nimal [another fellow villager, a frequent visitor to the office who aspires to be the office typist] tells the client that he could get him the book without the letter from the GS. Upon hearing this, Chandra is annoyed and says, 'What will that man think of me? I who work in this office had to turn him away while Nimal, who does not belong here, has agreed to help.' She asks Rodrigo not to exchange the ration book if Nimal brings the client back without a letter from the GS. Rodrigo agrees, but adds that if Nimal brings this case when he is out, Pediric, the other clerk in the Food Control Section, may handle it and perhaps do this favor for Nimal. Chandra then tells Rodrigo that she is not close enough to Pediric to ask him not to help Nimal. Kamala, who has listened to this conversation, says 'Why should Nimal undertake to do such a thing in the first place? He is not really part of this office.'

If an official successfully negotiates a transaction for a client, the latter should respond in one of the following two ways. One way is to openly acknowledge the favor and pat the official on the back, as in this case:

Case Seven. Mrs. Perera, a personal friend of the AGA and a member of the same caste, brings an application for a bag of cement and immediately receives the permit for it. Within a two-week period, she has come for a permit for white cloth (required for a burial) and, another time, to obtain a new rice ration book. As she leaves, she turns to me (the only other person in the room besides the AGA) and says, 'Because of our AGA mahattaya [gentleman], not only can we now get things done quickly but also we can also come in and make a request without fear or hesitation.' The AGA, obviously pleased, adds with a smile, 'Yes, I try to meet the demands of my job as quickly as possible. We are doing a social service, no?'

This is usually the case in situations where the basis of transactions is friendship or some degree of kinship dependent upon bilateral exchange and balanced reciprocity. The second accepted method for showing appreciation is through the use of certain forms of 'gifts.' To this category belongs the often jokingly worded request for a cup of tea or a meal. Unlike other forms of gifts, these requests to reciprocate a favor are, in fact, requests on the part of the official to be treated as an equal.[11] It can be concluded that this is an extension of the idea of commensality as symbolizing equality in a caste-based society. Token thanks are appreciated but not obligatory, the obligations of the transaction being met in different social contexts. But in the case of a 'gift,' overt or covert pressure is brought to bear upon the client to make him meet his part of the obligation. Thus,

----

Case Eight. Simon brings a plate of biscuits (i.e., cookies) and sweets, and serves the members of the office. The AGA asks him what the occasion is and Simon replies that Kamala is celebrating because she has passed the Grade II exam, which determines promotion within the clerical service. Chandra overhears this and asks Simon in a low voice, 'Is that really

so?' The latter denies his earlier assertion and, indicating a
middle-aged male client who is standing by the door, says, 'He
brought them.' Chandra asks what Simon did by way of services
to merit this, and the latter replies 'Nothing in particular,
but a lot of little things over time, and when he came by today,
Kamala and I told him hämadāma nikan ata vanavanā enavā [every
day he comes empty handed], and so he went and brought us these
eats.' This was a not-so-subtle way of indicating that it was
high time that the client met his obligations or risk future
favors being withheld. Kamala ends the conversation by adding,
'If clients always bring us things like this, how much more can
we do for them?'

In relation to the upper or lower ranks, each official is
formally subordinate or superordinate, but each official's
sentiments about his position make him feel inferior to none.
Self-esteem as revealed in official capacity is inexorably
intertwined with personal status. Therefore, when Chandra is
about to address a letter to the GA, she says, 'I don't know why
people address letters to him as disāpatitumā [GA -- Honored
Sir]. It should simply be disāpati [GA]; after all,...why
should we 'Sir' him in a letter?' Unless one is in the presence
of a superior, an official is not bound to defer to him in
formal communication. In a similar vein, in the absence of the
staff assistant, senior clerk Lionel acts for him. The phone
rings -- the only phone in the entire office is on the AGA's
desk -- and Lionel answers it. He returns, having put the
receiver aside, and tells Chandra that the call is for Sirima,
another of the clerks. Looking towards the latter's seat, he
sees that it is vacant. Chandra tells Lionel that Sirima is
having her breakfast in the tea room at the rear of the
building). Lionel pretends not to hear this, looks around
further and repeats, 'It is for Sirima and she is not around; we
cannot tell her if she is not in her seat.' Officially, it is
either Simon's or Jamis's (the other minor employee) job to

deliver messages, and Lionel feels that it is beneath his dignity to do the job of a petty official for a counterpart of his. Chandra listens without comment and Lionel goes back to his seat, leaving the phone off the hook. Chandra says to me, 'Why should I deliver the message if he can't? After all, I am also like him, no? Giving the message to Sirima because of personal friendship is something else.' Meanwhile, the AGA returns to his desk and, seeing the phone off the hook, puts the receiver back in place.

Both of these cases illustrate a single point: whether the relationship in question is that of the GA and the clerk (clearly superior-inferior), or that of peers (like Lionel, Chandra and Sirima, who are all clerks), no one in any way considers himself/herself inferior to the others. This is symbolized by the fact that each official has his physical niche in the office, his 'seat.' To sit in another's seat is to usurp the latter's position and the power and prestige it carries; this is a cause for resentment. A usurper must show some degree of compensatory behavior. For example, in the absence of the SA, either Lionel or Shelton acts for him. While Shelton does this from his own seat (using the SA's place only if the need arises), Lionel makes it a point to occupy the SA's seat whenever the opportunity arises. This occupation of the SA's seat, especially by Lionel, arouses ridicule from the others. They frequently tease Shelton in the presence of Lionel -- as a hint to the latter -- by asking him why he is reluctant to take the SA's vacant seat. Shelton smilingly replies, "Those high places are not for me, I keep away from them." But Lionel does not keep away, and the result is hostility:

Case Nine. The Additional GA calls to speak with a clerk who does land work, and Lionel makes the following retort, 'What kind of land work? I don't do everything' [he shares this responsibility with Rosilin, who is absent on this day]. Lionel goes to the phone and returns. He tells the SA, 'The Additional

GA wants to know what we did about the acquisition of Retreat
Estate; this is not my work. You better look there,' indicating
Rosilin's desk. The SA looks among Rosilin's files and
literally looks lost. Upon seeing this, Chandra helps him out,
and when she returns to her seat she says to me, 'Poor SA. Why
couldn't Lionel have found that file for him? He knows all
about land work. He is so reluctant to help, but when the SA is
not there, of course, he is always willing to take his seat.'

An official's status, in order to convey meaning in the
context of the impinging cultural environment, has to be acted
out in a visible fashion. The image of a person's official
status bears upon his self-image (cf. Mead 1934, Bailey, 1971).
Reputation[12] as a good or bad person, depending on how
successfully an official plays his role vis-à-vis the client,
is crucial. Within the social environment of the small
community, reputation spreads by word of mouth. In the words of
a former GA, "In a community that loves hyperbole everything
seems larger than it is." The Sinhalese term for reputation,
prasiddhiya, is synonymous with "publicity." In order to
maintain a good reputation with either a client or the high
echelons, an official must have what is termed "the personal
touch." To cultivate a positive self-image, one must build
trust, establish one's personal integrity, and cultivate the
honda hita [good will] of others. Creating a good impression
with the community through one's official acts also earns
religious merit. Given the face-to-face nature of Sri Lankan
society, failure to maintain a good reputation through positive
acts leads to embarrassment and loss of face. In Sinhala there
are several ways of describing this condition: muhuna balanna
bä [cannot look one in the face], numbuva giyā [prestige is
lost], or sāyama giyā [the paint has been washed off]. Loss of
face has obvious status consequences. The Additional GA says:

It is up to us to win the confidence of the
community and this is a matter of personal
touch. When you first come, they [clients]
are watchful. They wait to see what kind of
person you are, how you deal with people,
whether you are kind and compassionate.
These are fundamental concepts in Buddhism.
Having established this reputation with a few
members of the community, even if you don't
have personal contact with the others,[13]
the word will spread....Depending on how you
handle your first clients, your reputation is
established and very soon others will start
coming to you or avoiding you.

The same note is struck in the following case.

Case Ten. A grama sevaka who has served in the same region
throughout his career will be retiring next year. This is an
index of his popularity, since an unpopular GS would at some
time have been transferred. There are no complaints recorded in
his personal file. An opinion survey conducted in a randomly
selected group of residents in his division revealed that
community opinion of this GS has been consistently positive,
affirming the following point: 'He is a good man, he helps
everyone, he never asks for a bribe.' The GS's own
interpretation for his self-acknowledged popularity was as
follows:

It is important to cultivate the honda hita
of the community and this I do by treating all
alike, irrespective of race or caste or
whether they are rich or poor. I show concern
for the welfare of the people by getting to
know them personally, as far as possible or
else through others by reputation, by talking
to others and generally getting around. I

like to help improve the lot of the people in
my division. On my own initiative I have
obtained social assistance and welfare for the
needy by tracking them down. After all,
helping others is an act of merit (pina)
according to my religion [Buddhism].

In both of these cases the impersonal working situation of
the official is personalized and made more compatible with the
demands of the cultural environment. That helps the clients.
The motive for wanting to gain acceptance in the community
through the personal touch varies from a desire for self-esteem
and prestige to the accumulation of religious merit. In neither
instance do the rules of an impersonal bureaucracy prevail.

In his daily routine, an official is thrown into close
contact with other officials. They are a primary group. As
officials working in the same office they are linked by
face-to-face relationships and comprise a brotherhood.[14]
Being in such close contact, they must look each other in the
face, and all actions are controlled so that the capacity to
look others in the face is not endangered. To look a man in the
face is to recognize the bond of group solidarity and reciprocal
obligations. Failure to meet such obligations means loss of
face in the eyes of the others, and the offender then feels that
he cannot look them in the face.

During the weeks prior to the general elections, the
officials in the AGA's office were anxious to know beforehand
where they would be assigned election duty, i.e., officiating at
the polling booths. They approached the election officials
(also part of the kachcheri administrative complex), but failed
to find out their assignments. This event was described thus by
the SA: 'These days the people in the elections branch won't
look us in the face (muhuna balannet nä). They pretend not to
know us (anduranne nä).' The implication is that if the
election officials looked them in the face and thereby

recognized them, they would be compelled to divulge the assignments, while for security reasons these were kept confidential until the last minute.

While it is possible to avoid looking in the face of those who are in a different office, even within the same administrative complex, it is not possible to do so where the officials work in a single physical space, such as the AGA's office. In this setting, official interactions are formally polite and social distance is maintained. Peers, superordinates, and subordinates address each other as Mr. Silva, Miss Sirima, etc., except that subordinates also address their superiors as "Sir." Interactions outside the office are confined to ceremonial visits at funerals, births, and weddings, in that order of importance. Such visits are considered necessary to maintain solidarity and good will in the office. When clerk Joyce's elder brother died, her colleagues visited the house where the corpse was lying prior to burial, and again on the day of the funeral. They also contributed money for a wreath. When Sirima gave birth, the other females in the office visited her. When Sarath, the rural development officer, got married, only those who were invited (his close associates, male and female) jointly bought the wedding gift. Solidarity in times of loss and sorrow rather than on occasions for happiness is regarded as crucial to the successful maintenance of face-oriented behavior within the bureaucracy. The underlying assumption is that "you do for others what you would wish to have done for yourself."

Interactions within the office are characterized by the same principle of balanced reciprocity. One does not ask a favor of another unless one is certain that one can repay it in some form in the near future (this is largely confined to the exchange of services), and that one's request will not be turned down. In both cases this could mean loss of face for the one making the request. The concept used to designate such a situation is palvenavā [stink, stagnate, lose prestige].

Case Eleven. Chandra is ready to leave for home about 15
minutes before closing time, and I join her in her walk towards
the bus stop. As she approaches the door the SA accosts her and
says, 'Shall we go and talk to Pediric about that person's
ration book?' Chandra looks reluctant, shrugs her shoulders and
says, 'Even the AGA knows that client.' We leave and Rosilin,
who is also ready to leave, joins us. As we walk towards the
bus stop, Chandra says, 'That man [referring to the client
involved in the preceding conversation] is known to me. He is
from our village, he knows the SA and the AGA. He is the
chairman of our Village Council. You know, Kamala talks very
brusquely, and if you don't know her you may think that she is
scolding you. Now this man has come to her to get a license for
tapping toddy and she has spoken to him in her usual tone. He
has asked her whether she spoke so roughly because she got
scolded by her husband that morning. At this, Kamala became
very angry and told Pediric about it. When this client came to
get his rice ration book, Pediric refused to give it to him' [he
could not have legitimately refused; perhaps he postponed
issuing it]. 'This was at least two weeks ago and since then,
this client told me to inquire about it from Pediric. I asked
Pediric the other day and he said that he had to obtain a fresh
stock of rice ration books before he could issue one. This
happened two days ago, and since then he got a new stock of
books. This means that he has received fresh stocks twice, and
despite my asking him, he still did not give this client his
ration book. I don't know what that client must be thinking
about me...he must be thinking that I don't even consider a
request from a fellow villager. If I were to ask Pediric again,
he may do it and then say this and that, behind my back. Why
should I lose status (palvenavā)? We don't have to lose face to
someone from our own office and moreover to someone who is of
our own status (apē kanthoruwē api vagēma ekkenekugen pal venna
vädak nä ne). He comes to us and says, 'Do this quickly' for
someone known to him. How many income certificates have I

written for him? But when we want something from him, this is how he treats (<u>salakannē</u>) us.'

The implications of this case are numerous. The central theme is that Chandra made a request of Pediric and felt rejected when he did not treat her as she had treated him. To be rejected by a superior may be tolerable, but to be rejected by a peer is unpardonable. Fear of being rejected again explains her reluctance to go with the SA and talk to Pediric. At the same time she persuades herself that had she done so, he might have acceded to her request. But her lack of confidence and trust in Pediric is revealed in what she says about him. This case also has consequences for Chandra in terms of prestige and esteem in her village, because the client in question is no ordinary villager. Finally, it reveals the strength of Kamala's reciprocal links with Pediric and the weakness of Chandra's.

Related to the loss of face that results from being refused a favor by a fellow official, or the sense of inadequacy that results from being unable to help a known client, is the fear of being reprimanded in public by a senior official. This is tacitly understood as something one does not do. When it does happen, the official who does the reprimanding becomes unpopular, as illustrated by the following case.

<u>Case Twelve</u>. The AGA opens a file which has been placed before him, and looks perplexed. He calls Chandra and asks whether she is A or A1 -- clerks being categorized by the subjects they handle -- and she replies that she is the former. The AGA then says, 'Now look at this file. Remember, child, that you as the subject clerk should first minute this and then give it to me so that I will know what it is all about. When I was clerk in the land branch, I used to send files to my boss with the phrase 'submitted for approval.' Then one day my boss sent the file back to me and said, 'Go through this and tell me what I should do.' I learned my lesson that day. These days no

one knows these things because no one tells them about it. How
can you join the Ceylon Administrative Service if you don't know
the answer to such practical questions as how to submit a file?
I am telling you this like a father. You are an intelligent
child and you must learn to do things properly. So don't get
angry!' Chandra smiles, says that she is not angry, takes back
the file and returns it later, having minuted it properly.

This incident occurred in the morning, and at the end of the
day, as Chandra and I walked away from the office, she said to
me, 'This AGA is not like the earlier one. He was very simple
and kind. Even if we committed a mistake we had no fear of
being reprimanded. He never reprimanded us. In fact, he
himself would correct our mistakes. It is a great loss to us
that he was transferred from the office...and he was not even a
ranker like this one' [direct recruits to the CAS having more
prestige than clerks who are promoted to it].

Having been reprimanded in my presence, however mildly, resulted
in embarrassment for Chandra. She expressed her annoyance,
despite her earlier assertion that she was not angry, by subtly
implying that Douglas was a bad man rather than a bad AGA.

Within the context of the actual transaction of a favor, the
formal terms of address are informalized. Kamala would have
referred to Pediric not as Mr. Pediric Samarapala, but simply
with the diminutive Samare. In addition, terms of address are
further informalized by the borrowing and use of kin terms based
on sex and age. In making a request from Chandra, Pediric calls
her 'nangi' [younger sister] or 'Chandra nangi' [younger sister
Chandra]. Similarly, in making a request from Simon, Chandra
refers to him as malli [younger brother]. On the other hand,
Shelton was referred to as "Uncle Shelton" by Chandra, Pediric,
Kamala and Simon. Shelton, Lionel, and AGA Douglas were the
only older males (i.e., in their 50s) in this office of 15
persons. Lionel was always referred to by everyone as Mr.
Lionel (Lionel mahattaya). This is indicative of their attitude

towards him: he is an object of sarcasm and ridicule due to his exaggerated notions about his own self-importance. Neither the AGA nor his predecessor Somapala was referred to by a familiar term, kin or otherwise. The relationship between the AGA and the others is one of authority, and the only correct term of address for him is "Sir." Again, those who were about the same age (mid-20s to mid-30s) and who were female never resorted to kin terms, but addressed each other by their first names, and were similarly addressed by males in the same category.

On the other hand, males of about the same age would, besides referring to each other by abbreviated versions of their last names, also use the kinship term maccan in negotiating a transaction. Thus, the AGA tells a client who demands cement, "Sam is a brother officer and he came in the other day and said, 'maccan, give me a bag of cement,' and even then I could not oblige him, so how can I give it to you?" The implication here is that, had he cement, he would certainly have obliged the man who called him maccan (to whom he is also a maccan), and this means that he truly has no cement to give. In Sinhalese kinship, the term maccan is based on massina [cross-cousin or brother-in-law]; a person who addresses another as maccan takes the friendly role of cross-cousin or brother-in-law. According to AGA Douglas, the use of this term signifies cordiality and trust between the participants in the interaction. Sinhalese folklore relates how a pearl fishermen diving into the deep sea gives the end of his lifeline to his maccan. When this term is used in transactions either between officials, or (as discussed later) between official and client, it carries the underlying assumption that as one's maccan, the person to whom one is making the request will do his best to honor it.

This chapter is primarily an examination of the values associated with selfhood and the significance of why one must not be too accessible. We have also examined the relevance of culturally derived ideas of status, prestige and reputation to the maintenance of the bureaucratic persona, and ultimately the ways in which these ideas of selfhood are reinforced or undermined by interactions between fellow officials or between official and client. In the next chapter we turn to the topic of access: how clients gain (or fail to gain) access to officials and to the goods and services which they control.

FOOTNOTES

1. The three "ideal types" of legitimate authority as defined by Weber (1969:328) are: (a) legitimacy based on rational grounds, resting on the legality of normative rules and the right of those elevated to authority under such rules to issue commands; (b) legitimacy based on traditional grounds, resting in the belief in the sanctity of immemorial tradition and the legitimacy of those exercising authority under them; and (c) legitimacy based on charismatic grounds, resting on the character of an individual person and of the order revealed or ordained by him.

2. This Republican Constitution has since been replaced.

3. Warnapala (1974:221-22) questions the impartiality of the PSC.

4. The concept of "bureaucratic personality" is derived from Merton (1969:255).

5. To quote Bailey, "...where everyone knows about everyone else, or if they do not actually know about a particular person, they know who will be able to talk about him. These are face-to-face societies" (1971:4).

6. In discussing his pattern variables, Parsons defined particularism as follows:
    Culture aspect -- the normative pattern which obliges an actor in a given situation to give priority to particular relations...over generalized attributes, capacities or performance standards. Personality aspect -- a need disposition on the part of the actor to be guided by criteria of choice particular to his own and the object's position in an object-relationship system rather than criteria defined in generalized terms. Social system aspect -- the role expectation that, in qualification for memberships and decisions for differential treatment, priority will be given to standards which assert the primacy of the values attached to objects by their particular relations to the actor's properties ...as over against their general universally applicable class properties (1962:82).

7. Parsons states that universalism, in its cultural aspect, is
    ...the normative pattern which obliges an actor in a given situation to be oriented toward objects in the light of the object's

possession of properties...which have a
particular relation to the actor's own
properties....Personality aspect -- a need
disposition on the part of the actor in a
given situation to respond toward objects in
conformity with a general standard rather than
in the light of their possession of properties
...which have a particular relation to the
actor's own. Social system aspect -- the rule
expectation that, in qualifications for
memberships and decisions for differential
treatment, priorities will be given to
standards defined in completely generalized
terms, independent of the particular
relationship of the actor's own statuses...to
those of the object (Ibid.).

8. Bailey states that "Impersonal relationships are those
in which the actors wear a mask. The intention of the mask is
to seal this relationship from any other relationship or
attribute or responsibility which each of the actors may have,
either towards one another..." (Ibid., p. 290).

9. A Householders List is an individual record of names of
persons, particulars of citizenship (i.e., whether individuals
are citizens of Sri Lanka by descent or by registration), and
the serial numbers of the rice ration books in each household.
Among other things, this list is essential as proof of one's
citizenship, to exercise one's right to vote in parliamentary
elections, to prove one's residency in a particular region, and
for legal ownership of property.

10. Goffman (1959:22) defines performance as "all the
activity of an individual which occurs during a period marked by
his continuous presence before a particular set of observers
which has some influence on the observers." Bailey (1971:2-24)
gives an anthropological analysis of this concept.

11. According to Mauss, "To refuse to give, or the failure
to invite is...a refusal of friendship and intercourse"
(1966:11).

12. Bailey states that
A man's reputation is not a quality that he
possesses but rather the opinion which other
people have of him....My reputation is one of
the factors which control the way I can
interact with other people and manipulate them
to gain whatever ends I have in view.
Therefore only the opinions of those with
whom I am likely to interact are important to
me....As the importance of one's reputation
diminishes the intensity of interaction

> also diminishes....[In small communities]
> there is a fund of common knowledge about all
> the members of the community, and...it is not
> too difficult for anyone in the community to
> have access to it. This fund, in fact, is
> made up of reputations (Ibid., p. 4).

13. It is interesting to note how, on one occasion, the GA
reacted to a client. When ordered to pay a fine for failing to
license his gun, the client claimed ignorance on the grounds
that he did not realize his gun was not licensed, and said that
on the date for licensing he had been taken ill and
hospitalized. When appealing to the GA to reduce the fine, he
said, "nodanna minihata anukampā karala [show compassion for the
ignorant]." The GA's answer was "nodanna minihat dänaganne ōnä
[the ignorant should learn]."

14. This is analogous to Cohen's concept of cousinhood or
brotherhood (1974:43).

CHAPTER 4

Accessibility:

The Known Face and the Unknown

In this chapter, we look in more detail at the ways in which
the impersonal facade of the official becomes personalized. Our
first question deals with who has access to the official, and
what procedures are followed to gain access.

In the words of a former GA, "the way an officer treats a
member of the public is based on who he is rather than what he
has come for. If you say that you are so and so, then the
official will get up from his chair, walk to the relevant
section of the office and get your job done, himself." The
client who is treated in this manner is called the "known face":

Case Thirteen. AGA Douglas is acting for his counterpart in
the neighboring division. A client arrives and both recognizes
and is recognized by the AGA. The latter asks the former the
reason for his visit, and the client says that, though he has
applied for 25 bags of cement, he has only received two so far.
An acute shortage of cement has necessitated rationing, and this
client has appeared at the height of the crisis; still, the AGA
says to him, 'Now, there is enough cement; you go and ask the SA
to give you at least five more.' The AGA calls the SA, telling
him, 'You had better give him five more bags.' The SA
reluctantly goes to the clerk who handles cement permits.

A few minutes later, both of them come to the AGA, and the
clerk tells him, 'Sir, there are 75 applications and only 200
bags are left.' The AGA orders him to give out the cement. He
then turns to me and says, 'In my division I have no problem. I
give what I have to brother officers and known faces. We can
count on them to support us in the future, no? So I grant them
their requests. As for the others, these unknown people, I just
tell them I don't have any. I ask them to go away and come back

later; this is my policy. Also,' he says to me humorously, 'by
helping these people I will get some merit in my next birth,'
for the Buddhist ideal of helping one's fellow man, especially
the poor and helpless, is in practice taken to mean helping
one's own kind.

Helping "known faces" is useful in another sense as well:
'Because I know them, they won't try to cheat me. Take the case
of cement permits -- I know who makes a genuine request and who
is a black marketeer.' The AGA's typical reaction to a client's
request for cement would be, 'How can you build on the premises
where you live? You are not the owner of the building. By
municipal law, only the owner is entitled to renovate or enlarge
a building.' The AGA continues, 'Also, they know that if they
do cheat, I will discover it sooner or later. Because they know
me, they will not force my hand on an unwarranted act or make
impossible demands. On my part, I go out of my way to help them
and they come to me confident that I will not let them down.'

The above case clearly reveals the dynamics of the formally
rational bureaucracy in action within the Sri Lankan
sociocultural environment. In a situation centering on
official-client interaction, where the normative demand is that
of authority relationships based on rational impersonalism, the
pragmatic adaptation is one of non-rational personalism with
relationships based on personal trust and confidence.

The Known Face:
Kinsman, Friend, Fellow Villager

The phrase "known face" covers several social categories
which may overlap. It may refer to a kinsman or a friend, or to
a person from one's village. The following combinations may
occur: kinsman [therefore also a fellow caste member] who is
also a friend and fellow villager; kinsman and fellow villager;

kinsman and friend; kinsman and fellow villager; friend, whether
Sinhalese, Muslim, or Burgher; friend who is also a fellow
villager; fellow villager, whether Sinhalese, Muslim, or
Burgher. Transactions between officials and all but the last
category of clients are expressed in a kinship idiom.[1]

With the known face, the formal front becomes personalized
in the following ways: a smile of recognition, address by
personal names or kin terms, and preliminary small talk followed
by speedy coping with (or bending of) the normative rules of the
system, by the official on behalf of the client. AGA Douglas
says, "My policy is to bend the rules given the practicalities
of the situation. Necessity knows no law. I circumvent the law
for known faces and thereby do them a service." On the other
hand, it could result in the personal recognition of the client
by the official, but with a stress on rules and an emphasis of
how difficult it is to do this particular favor, before finally
undertaking the transaction.

Favors requested and granted are of two types: goods --
scarce commodities such as rationed cement; and services -- such
as the transfer of a rice ration book from one regional
cooperative to another. With the first type of favor, since
demand exceeds supply, the distribution of these scarce
commodities is very important. According to AGA Douglas, "I try
to accommodate known peoples and never say no to them, so that
they will have a good word for me. It is true that I may not be
able to satisfy all the known faces every time, but I have
helped them all, at one time or another." Thus, when the AGA
receives a request for cement from a "brother" (i.e., an
official from another government department), he promptly
accedes to it with the following statement: "If we cannot help
each other in at least something like this, of what use is our
relationship?" A friend who is also a known face with similarly
given priority is told, "You are a good friend of mine and I
have to support you." Meanwhile, a local fish dealer named
Carolis arrives at the office accompanied by another client.

Walking up to AGA Douglas, he tells the client, "This is our
aiya [elder brother]"; turning to the AGA, he says "Aiya, you
know this person, don't you?" for he and the AGA are from the
same caste and village as Carolis. "He needs a couple of bags
of cement to complete building his kitchen before the festival,"
referring to the Sinhala New Year. The AGA reacts by saying,
"Yes, now you come and address me as aiya, but when you come to
see your aiya can't you at least bring a santōsam?" This
literally means "happiness," but as used here it is meant as a
gift, specifically of some fish. He goes on to say, "The only
favor you have done to me is when I go to the market, you sell
me the fish which is priced for Rs. 6.75 a pound for Rs. 5.75."
Carolis replies, "At least I reduced the price by Rs. 1/. Is
that not enough?" The AGA, in granting the request, was doing
so for a known face.

It may also happen that a client comes to the AGA with an
application for cement, only to be told that there is no more
available. To this, the client responds that it is a request
for a funeral, that is, to build a grave. Such requests are
given high priority, because of the belief that the dead have
the right to a decent resting place -- a cemented grave -- and
also because few clients would manufacture such a reason, even
if they badly needed the cement for some nefarious purpose.[2]
The AGA looks at the application and tells the client that this
form indicates the funeral has already taken place, meaning that
the client has somehow already procured the cement. The client
replies that he borrowed three of the necessary five bags from
his neighbor, who had obtained it to build a lavatory and who is
demanding its immediate return. The AGA replies that the client
should have come to him first, rather than going to the
neighbor; the client says that this would have been impossible,
since the funeral took place on a weekend, when the office was
closed. The AGA says that the client should have come to his
home: "Many people do so, and I have a set of applications at
home for this purpose. We are required to reside within our

division to handle emergencies like this. Now you will have to
wait until I get fresh stocks." The client persists, saying,
"Now my neighbor and I will come to blows." The AGA relents,
saying "Can you at least bring the receipt from the cemetery to
prove that the burial in fact took place?" The client says that
this is not possible since the burial was done in a private
garden rather than the public cemetery. Finally, the AGA
capitulates, saying, "You are a man known to me (aňdurana
minihek), someone whom I meet constantly, so how can I say no?
I will give you two bags now, and you may get the third later."

By chance, a few minutes later, another client comes with
the same problem, only to be told by the AGA that "You should
have come on the day of the funeral; now there is no cement for
you." As this client leaves, the AGA tells me that he is down
to his last 30 bags of cement, and so must be very careful of
how he disburses them. Soon afterwards, Douglas is approached
for cement by a known face who is a Muslim. Douglas says, "Of
course, I must oblige you, we are known people, and neither
yesterday nor today but for generations. We are like brothers,
my grandfather knew your grandfather...." The client and the
AGA are from the same neighborhood, the client's father and the
AGA were childhood friends, and the client's father is a
well-known businessman and thus an ally in future transactions.

Unlike transactions involving goods, those centered upon
services cost the official little, because he does not have to
decide priorities and thereby risk antagonizing some clients. A
client who comes to get his rice ration book changed from the
taxpayer type to the non-taxpayer variety is greeted by the AGA
in the following manner: "You are a good friend of my friend
Neville and you are also my kinsman; it is a simple thing to
change the ration book." While the client is seated in the
AGA's office, reminiscing with him about old times, Simon takes
the client's documents to the Food Control Section and completes
the transaction. Exchanging a rice ration book, unlike giving
out a bag of cement, is not a difficult task; still, the

sociocultural significance of the interaction is important. The
client is able to get his new ration book without the delay
involved in dealing with the official in charge of food control,
to whom he is an unknown. In the narrow sense, there is
conformity in these transactions to the norms of the
bureaucracy: the client who needs cement has to fill out a
permit and those who need to exchange rice ration books must
make formal applications as well. But in spirit, so to speak,
the official normative structure of formality-impersonality
gives way to personalism.

The official depends on the good opinion of his primary
group -- his kānde [following], which includes nā [relations],
mitra [friends], aṅdurana [known] -- to preserve a satisfactory
image of himself. One must treat (salakannē) a member of one's
kānde in order to be reciprocally treated by him. The principle
of salakannē carried to its extreme can be a source of tension
for the official. He cannot refuse to treat his kānde without
losing face. Therefore on occasion he is forced, against his
wishes, to say yes to a request. AGA Somapala repeatedly said
that he wished he could be transferred to a remote region so
that he could escape from his endless obligations to the kānde
which forced him to bend the rules too often.[3] On the other
hand, AGA Douglas would often tell a client who was a known face
that "I have accommodated you, I wish you would not press me
further." Clerk Chandra, meanwhile, says that

Case Fourteen. "It is impossible to cope with these cement
permits. Everyone from my village comes hoping to get cement
through me. How many times can I got to the AGA for favors?
Maybe three times, but no more. I told this client Sirapala
that maybe the SA will help him as he is a kinsman of the SA and
myself," the client being Chandra's fellow villager and kinsman,
but only a fellow caste member of the SA, and one with whom he
does not meet frequently. "When I get a permit for one, the
word spreads and a lot of others come. I have told them not to

spread the word that I helped them. One should help if one can, but how many times can I go to the AGA? They don't realize that I cannot do these things and they should know not to ask me. Just because I work in this office they think that I can do anything."

The following themes emerge: Somapala is placed in the dilemma of having to decide between the norms of the bureaucracy and those of the kānde; he hopes for a transfer to another area. Douglas, while not denying the validity of the claims of the kānde, is obviously setting limits to the demands made by them. Finally, Chandra is unable to meet the demands of the community on her own, and resents the fact that repeated favors in turn place her under obligation to (or arouse the fear of being refused by) another official. The concern for reputation is typified by the following case:

Case Fifteen. A client asks Chandra to get him a permit to tap toddy. She agrees, but as he leaves, Chandra tells me, 'He is a neighbor of mine. Recently, his house was robbed and his mother has spread the word that when they screamed for help, none of the neighbors came to their aid. We are their closest neighbors and if either my father or my elder brother had heard their cries, they would have gone to help. On the day after that, they borrowed our lamp and my brother went over and slept at their place to keep them company. Now his mother goes around saying that we did not respond to their cry for help because we are jealous of their riches. Really, I should not help this person.' She then proceeds to do just the opposite.

This type of reputation-oriented behavior is most common between the GS and members of his division:

Case Sixteen. A GS complains to the AGA about a gang of illicit liquor dealers in his division, who are also running an illegal gambling den. The GS says, 'I made a complaint to the police and moved aside -- <u>ayinakaṭa</u> <u>unā</u> [i.e., he only made the complaint but did not actively initiate any action against them] -- because I cannot be looking into the faces of these people, I will be isolated, they will seek revenge on me (<u>apata</u> <u>bǟ</u> <u>nē</u> <u>muhuna</u> <u>nobalā</u> <u>inṇa</u>, <u>api</u> <u>tani</u> <u>venavā</u>, <u>ē</u> <u>minissu</u> <u>vavira</u> <u>karanavā</u>).' The next day two clients appear before the AGA and one says, 'This is regarding the complaint that GS made to you in which he said that he raided an illicit gambling den and that the persons who ran it refused to stop their activity, even after being ordered to do so by the GS. This man here,' he says, indicating the other client, 'is the one who ran it, and he has something very confidential to say to you.' The AGA has listened to this man, who is speaking in a barely audible tone and who has a conspiratorial look on his face. He then says, "Okay," and calling Simon to his office, says, 'Now don't admit anyone into my office. I am conducting an inquiry.'

The first client leaves, and the alleged owner of the gambling den remains behind. Moving closer to the AGA, he whispers into his ear. The AGA takes up a pen and says, 'Okay, now,...you are Samson?' The client nods yes, and the AGA continues, 'Now you admit that you ran this gambling den either on a <u>tovil</u> [a traditional exorcistic ritual] or a funeral day?' The client admits that he did so. 'In that case,' the AGA says, 'to begin with, we will have to take action against you for doing this illegal activity. Do you realize this?' The client sheepishly says that he does, and the AGA goes on to say, 'Okay, you had this gambling den. Was it on a <u>tovil</u> or funeral day?' The client reaffirms that it was, and the AGA asks what happened. The client says, 'This <u>grama</u> <u>sevaka</u> came and drank at my place,' and the AGA asks how much he drank. 'About two drams, and then he asked me for a bribe in return for letting me continue with the gambling.' The AGA makes a note of this and says, 'You know that this GS can get dismissed from service for this.' At this, the client looks alarmed and says, 'We don't want to do something like that to the <u>grama</u> <u>sevaka</u> <u>rālahāmy</u> [the latter term being an honorific].' The AGA replies, 'If what you say here is factual, then you will have to sign this.' He indicates the statement he has taken and says, 'Then we will have a really formal inquiry.' The client asks if it will be in the presence of the GS in question, and the AGA says that it will: 'He will be there with his lawyers and you should be there with witnesses. Then we will have a formal inquiry. Can you substantiate what you have just told me and which I have noted down?' The client looks proccupied and says, faintly and hesitantly, 'Okay.'

At this, the AGA asks if the client has with him identification to prove that he is indeed Samson; the client says that he does not. The AGA says, 'That's okay, you sign this and we will have the inquiry.' The client signs and leaves. As he walks out, the first client comes back and says to the AGA, 'What he said should be very confidential." The latter replies, "Of course, how can what he said go out of here?' The client then leaves.

This case took place on the 25th of May and my field work ended on the 30th of July of that same year. Within this time, the promised inquiry was not held. But one can be sure that had it been held, the plaintiff would not have made an appearance on the appointed day. On the other hand, in the absence of identification it is possible that it was in fact not Samson who made the complaint, and that the real Samson might appear and deny having made the complaint. These are common strategies employed in petition hearings.

Not anticipating a formal face-to-face inquiry, what the plaintiff hoped to achieve through his complaint was punishment for the GS, even at the risk of admitting his own guilt in the matter of running the gambling den. On the other hand, what the plaintiff said could have been true, and the GS might actually have asked for a bribe. Having failed in this attempt, he might have complained to the police and then to the AGA. Whatever the truth, the plaintiff was concerned with keeping himself out of sight and was alarmed at the prospect of confronting the GS at an inquiry. In the same way, the GS remembers that he has to keep "looking into the faces of these people."

The Known Face:
The Socially Powerful and Well-Known

Another type of known face is the public figure. This may be an individual who is part of a known family, usually of feudal aristocratic origins or hāmus, or who is of a manorial or valavva family. While this group no longer exercises direct political power, it still retains social prestige. Often such people do not appear in person to carry out a transaction. Instead, they send their chauffeur, who is recognized and attended to by the official. The chauffeur may bring a personal letter for the AGA in which his master makes the request. In any case, the transaction is speedily attended to.

The relationship between the official and such a client is reversed. Situationally, the relationship remains one of official superiority and client subordination, but from the cultural perspective, the official is in the lower position. For him, however, such transactions further enhance his social prestige. These clients were once authority figures and socially prominent personages; thus the official can make it known in the community that he granted a favor he was asked by such an eminent person. In the public eye, it establishes a reciprocal relationship between the traditional elite and the official, who is typically of rural or middle class background, thus signaling equality.

The Unknown Client

The unknown client is likely to view the bureaucracy as follows: "Our bureaucracts are a set of omnipotent gods whom we have to worship. We cannot get anything done unless we crawl on our knees to their feet. If you go to a government office you will be convinced of the truth of the statement." This is from a letter published in the _Ceylon_ _Daily_ _News_ on May 6, 1977. The paper's editor, on October 7, 1976, had also written that "...each person who has dealings with the public servant will have his or her own tale of the scowls and frowns, the grunts and barks he or she has experienced. Such experience now forms part of the popular folklore." To a client who is not a known face, the bureaucratic persona of the official is indeed most formidable. This leads to a ruthless overemphasis of administrative rules. The very look of an unknown individual can antagonize an official. But there are mitigating devices.

The Passive Helpless Client

One type of client treated with more consideration is one who behaves like a feudal vassal. Often poor, unkempt and old, such clients wait outside the office door until opening time, and are then hesitant to approach the officials. When they do come forward, they have a servile demeanor and often address the officials as "lord" or hāmuduruvō.[4] They pose no threat to the inflated status/image of the official, and in fact they function as ego-boosters.

Officials feel an obligation to treat these people as considerately as if they were known faces. They are said to be helpless or asaranaya; one should thus feel sorry, pavu, for them and try to help them. They are generally petitioning for social welfare or relief during emergencies, or at times land, as in the following case:

Case Seventeen. AGA Somapala calls a meeting of grama
sevakas and rural development officers to decide on how to
allocate the 20 acres of land which remain for distribution
under the Land Reform Laws. Since the applicants are personally
known to these grassroots officials, the AGA inquires the latter
about the suitability of the applicants, that is, whether or not
they are landless and deserving. Of the 24 applicants who were
selected, 15 were females and the majority of these were
widows. The rest were selected on the grounds that they were
either ahimsaka [the innocent, i.e., someone who does not commit
aggression -- himsa] and asarana [helpless]. Those who gained
the approval of the village-level official and who thus received
land were the really helpless and non-aggressive, who truly
posed no threat to the official.

Finally, in the words of clerk Lionel,

> rājakariyata pera manussagatiya [humanity
> before duty]. We should always help our
> clients. Even if we cannot do so we should at
> least appear to do it and this will please
> them. I never treat anyone rudely.
> Otherwise when I am alone, I feel bad unless
> of course they are too much and then I get
> angry.

Those who are "too much" are those who either pose a threat to
the official's self-esteem or who arouse his ire.

The Circuit and the Petition

The techniques of the circuit and the petition are an
intrinsic part of the formal framework of the rational
bureaucracy in Sri Lanka. In the words of a former GA,

> The circuit in colonial times was a field
> visit by the GA, the purpose of which was to
> see in the field what one cannot visualize

from the office. The underlying assumption
was that unless the official is on the spot he
cannot picture the actual fact; no amount of
explanation by a client will do it. A man
will come and tell you that he and X own a
piece of land and that he gave half of it.
However, when I go and see it, it really is a
big rock, this so-called "half."

The circuit also originated in an era when, because of poor
communications, the administrative office was not easily
accessible to the client. In these circumstances, the circuit
became a way of taking the administration to the client.

Today in the Ganvälla kachcheri, the GA does not
undertake any circuits. This task is left largely in the hands
of his subordinates, the Additional GA and the AGAs of the
divisions. Unlike their predecessors, circuits nowadays last no
more than a few hours, and their purpose is merely to check on
something in the field: e.g., to inspect a completed irrigation
channel before making payments to the contractor. With the
construction of adequate roads and increased use of automobiles,
circuits are done not on horseback but in chauffeur-driven
Peugeots. Many of the ceremonial trappings of the circuit have
been lost as well. It is no longer an elaborately planned
expedition. It is neither frequent nor necessary. Furthermore,
the multitude of local-level politicians who have emerged in the
past few years now serve, to a large degree, as the channels of
communication between the community and the administrator; in
this sense they have usurped the omnipotent role of the
administrator, especially of the GA. The residual functions of
the circuit are left to lesser officials.

However marginal the nature of the circuit may be today, it
is still used by clients, especially of the unknown-helpless
category, to ventilate their grievances to the official. These
clients display an attitude of respect and awe reminiscent of
earlier circuits. When AGA Somapala made a circuit to check the

newly repaired irrigation channels in a nearby village, a crowd
of residents gathered to await his arrival; after the
inspection, they approached him about a variety of problems.
The AGA told these clients to come to his office to register
formal complaints about which he could take action. The AGA and
his party were then invited to tea at the home of a client.
Thus, the circuit remains a technique for venting grievances in
the eyes of clients who are hesitant to approach the
administrator in his office; it also serves to let these clients
experience what they view as the omnipotent and benevolent
authority of the administrator.

The origins of the petition[5] date back to the traditional
Sinhalese patrimonial administration (Pieris 1957). In the
words of a former GA,

> In the Sinhalese social organization there was
> the important position of the lekam [scribe,
> secretary], a literate person through whom an
> illiterate person can make a request through
> the written word -- a written note that was
> hand-carried -- a tundu källa. From the tundu
> källa emerged the petition (petsama).

Beginning as early as 1881, the format of the petition
changed considerably.[6] Appendix 1 is an example of a petition
dating from 1881, while a 1974 petition was worded as follows:

> Dear Sir,
>
> Complaint against the Grama Sevaka X.
>
> On the night of June 1, 1974, the Grama
> Sevaka of Walgalle in the company of Sgt.
> Piyadasa of Crime Branch of the Ganvälla
> Police entered my home. Both he and the
> police officer mentioned were smelling of
> liquor. This Grama Sevaka walked all over my
> house in search of a nephew of mine who was
> alleged to be wanted for questioning by the
> police.[7] This Grama Sevaka had no right to

enter my house as my residence does not fall
within his <u>Grama</u> <u>Sevaka</u> division and I object
to his invasion of my home by an official who
has no right whatsoever to do so under any
circumstances. This official abused me, my
wife and two unmarried daughters and
intimidated all of us, probably on the
strength of the fact that he has the
reputation of being belligerent.

I shall be grateful to your good self if
you would cause an inquiry to be held into
this and suitable action taken against this
official, should your good self deem it
necessary in the interests of preserving my
rights as a private individual.

Thanking you

I am Sir,

Yours faithfully

Sirisena de Silva

P.S. I have made representation to the
Hon. Minister of Public Administration too
regarding this matter.

Today the petition may vary widely, from a letter like that
quoted above, to a slip of paper on which a request is simply
written and signed, either in Sinhala or with a thumb
impression, the latter being more likely. The type of appeal
has changed from a "prayer," a "complaint," or a "statement of
grievances" to a protest. Petitions which in the past were
rejected as being of a "private nature and therefore beyond the
scope of..." (DNA27/274) form the bulk of today's petitions.
They range from complaints of incest or of marital infidelity to
personal antagonisms with fellow villagers. Like the circuit,
the petition has proved useful in running a rational
bureaucracy. By these means, both derived from an earlier
authority system, the client who is an unknown-helpess, without

useful connections, can make his grievances known. Those who do not have the ability to meet the commitments and reciprocal obligations involved in dealing with a politician resort to petitions. If the petition fails, the client may decide to approach a politician after all.

The petition and the professional petition writer (who, for a sum of Rs. 2/ would write a petition for an illiterate client) familiarize people with the ways of the modern bureaucracy. A former GA says that

> The petition writer with his knowledge of how to be specific on a request provides a service in cutting down a long-winded rigamarole. The client cannot think precisely, he is in distress and has only a vague idea of what is bothering him. He has no idea of what the heart of the problem [from the administrator's spective] is. The petition writer with his large experience is like the medicine man with his diagnosis. He is able to tell the client 'This is your problem, now do this.' The bureaucracy, with its emphasis on files and records, structures the situation for the client. It is a relief to have a document. Upon it you can make an order, get observations, pass it around, make a reply and it ends up in a file.

With the spread of literacy and the use of Sinhalese rather than English as the official language, more clients draft their own petitions today. Nevertheless, the petition writers are still at work.[8] The petition, whoever may write it, remains an invaluable survivor of an earlier system of administration which has been successfully incorporated into the modern system.

The Oral Component in Bureaucratic Transactions

A female client requests that AGA Douglas give her a rice ration book to replace one that she has lost. He says that she should first bring an affidavit from the GS of her division certifying that she has lost her original book. Douglas asks the client whether she has informed the GS of her loss, and she replies, "I <u>told</u> him." Douglas then says, "Merely <u>telling</u> him is not sufficient, you have to make a complaint (<u>kiyala</u> <u>bā</u>, <u>paminillak</u> <u>karanna</u> <u>onā</u>). Did he write down what you told him? You had better go back and bring that letter from the GS." The client leaves, and another client who has been listening to the conversation asks the AGA what would happen if the GS had not made note of her complaint. Douglas replies, "If she complained then he will remember the case. Then he can let me know about it in writing and then I can act upon his letter."

AGA Douglas typically tells known clients who have applied for cement permits and who complain to him that their applications have been ignored while other, later applications have been honored: "I did not know, no? You never came and <u>told</u> me. When we get our next quota of cement, I will grant your request. You had better come and remind me personally. Otherwise, there are so many others I have to consider, those who make a personal appeal to me, that I may forget your case."

To be effective, however, the oral request must be followed by a written one. Conversely, if a client has already gone through the written procedure, he can use the verbal approach to gain preference over other clients. In the latter event, however, as a former GA points out, "When an official tells a client 'you did not tell me' this not merely involves the telling itself but instead it means 'having known me [the official] earlier, why didn't you <u>tell</u> me?' It is the official's personal knowledge of the client which is important; you do things for people because you know them."

The Matter of Time

The normative framework of the Sri Lankan bureaucracy is set
according to Western notions of linear time. The AGA's office,
like all other government and non-government institutions in the
country, thus operates on a five-day week, Monday through
Friday. The typical working day runs from 8:15 a.m. to 4:15
p.m., with a lunch break from noon to 1 p.m. In matters of
administrative routine, the Administrative Regulations specify
the time limits within which an official should reply to
correspondence. Leave is calculated on the basis of a fixed
number of days. Administrative tasks are also time-structured.
For example, the exchange of rice ration books is stopped for
the first week of each month, to give the cooperatives a chance
to get their books in order. Similarly, timber permits are
granted for a fixed number of hours, depending on the distance
over which the timber must be transported.

Besides linear time, other types of time are used as well.
Among the Sinhala Buddhists, festivals -- both religious and
non-religious -- are used as markers. The Sinhala New Year is
the most important of these. It occurs in two phases: the old
year is celebrated, and then the new year proper is welcomed.
Between these two phases lies the neutral hour, nonakaté, during
which the spirit of nature hovers between death and birth. The
ritual of the New Year is so organized that man himself
symbolically shares the renewal of the power of nature: he
begins a fresh cycle of life and social activities.

These concepts are used by administrators as a mode of
communication with clients. For example, AGA Douglas, in the
face of an acute shortage of supplies and a flood of
applications for cement permits, tells a client, "I don't know
when I will get my next quota...there are others on the waiting
list before you, and I don't know when you will get yours. You
better come back after the Sinhala New Year and make your

transaction at a good time during the new year." On another
occasion, he tells a client to come after Vesak, the Buddhist
celebrations commemorating the Buddha's birth, death and
reaching of enlightenment. The important element in both cases
is that both festivals were still some time in the future when
these statements were made. Douglas himself said that the use
of festivals as markers -- rather than simply asking the client
to come back in six months, or admitting that he did not know
when the client might expect his request to be granted -- was
"to drive home to them in a language they understand, that I
cannot give them what they are asking for in the near future."

There is also the matter of religious time. Buddhists
believe in samsāra, the eternal cycle of birth-death-rebirth.
In the very distant future is the end of this cycle: nirvāna,
which an individual achieves through his good deeds in one
life. But achieving nirvāna is a remote concern for the average
person, who believes that the sins of his past lives have
predetermined that he be born many times over [karma] before
those sins are finally expiated. Samsāra contains a notion of
time as an external order, an endless cyclical pattern. These
notions are used in official-client interchanges. For example,
when the AGA must deal with a client upset over the fact that
his cement permit has not been granted, he says, "first come,
first served." The client then says that he submitted his
application two months ago, while his friend Weerasinghe, who
applied only last week, has already received his permit. The
AGA finally retorts, in a humerous vein, "Maybe it is your bad
karma that did it." At this point there is a noticeable change
in the client's demeanor; he backs away and leaves, saying, "I
will come back later."

We have seen that clients have access to officials according
to what sort of clients they are: If they are known faces,
access is relatively easy. If they are unknown, but present
themselves as helpless, they are well treated. While such
discrimination among types of clients is contrary to rational

bureaucratic procedures, it conforms with the demands of the culture and with the needs of the bureaucratic persona. We have seen that there are formal modes of application and formal procedures for access, among them the circuit and the petition. We have also noted that the cultural idioms of time (structural or religious) can be imposed on the linear arrangement of time proper in a bureaucracy by an official to justify, to a client, restrictions on access. The larger culture, in short, can be used both to open and to close the gate.

FOOTNOTES

1. Price discusses the significance of kinship in Ghanaian bureaucracy (1975:56-82).

2. The number of requests for cement for funerals quadrupled during this time. This prompted the AGA to report, "As soon as I announced that I had cement only for funerals, more people have started dying. If it is in the town I will know whether it is true or not. But in the interior there is no way of checking." Theoretically, the grama sevakas could verify these deaths, but it is practically impossible to expect them to do so in the absence of speedy communications between the AGA's office and the grama sevakas.

3. This is the only case which lends support to Faller's argument (1965) that the administrator in a semi-traditional society is necessarily placed in a situation of conflict when he must choose between carrying out his official tasks impartially and compromising his position by granting favors to kinsmen. Conflict exists not at the level of choice but at that stage when the official is unable to meet the constant demand for favors and thereby loses face in the eyes of the community.

4. On one such occasion the AGA, uncomfortable at being addressed in this manner, said flippantly, "Don't call me hāmuduruvō! Hāmuduruvō is in the temple." (This term is also used in Sri Lanka to refer to a Buddhist monk.)

5. This is similar to the description given by Katz and Danet (1966). According to them, the content of the appeals in petitions to the Israeli bureaucracy was influenced more by the normative basis of the organization than by the client's ability to offer his resources in exchange for those of the organization.

6. Wickremaratne (1970:213-32) gives a comprehensive discussion of the historical origins and functions of the petition, while Gunasekere, in his novel Petsama (1973), highlights its ramifications in a Sinhalese village.

7. The AGA's inquiry revealed that the petitioner's nephew had stolen articles worth 30,000 rupees from a tailoring shop, and was being sought by the police. The accused worked at a garage run by the petitioner, and the GS had accompanied the police on the latter's invitation solely to identify the accused, who is a resident of the grama sevaka's territorial division. During the search of the petitioner's house, 7,000 yards of the stolen material was discovered. The petitioner is considered a respectable man in the area, and this incident had resulted in loss of face for him; the petition is a consequence of this.

8. Traditionally, the petition writer was seated at a table outside the <u>kachcheri</u>. Today this role has been increasingly taken over by the proctor's clerks, i.e., those clerks who work in attorneys' offices in the vicinity of the <u>kachcheri</u>.

CHAPTER 5

Accessibility:
Strategies of the Unknown Client

Those who are not "in the brotherhood" and who are not known faces are the unknown. But they are not literally unknown, or, at least, they are not unknowable; on the contrary, the official can usually recognize this type of client and his or her status in society. Unknown clients are not those who are helpless; they are often prosperous, self-confident farmers or members of the urban middle class. But they are not a part of the traditional elite. Finally, no moral obligation is felt toward them, as in the case of the known face, and there is an implicit (at times explicit) expectation that favors granted to the unknown should be reciprocated in cash or in kind, before a second favor can be requested.

A client who enters the office with his head held high can be sure of an unfavorable response from the official. Clients who enter without waiting for the peon to usher them in are asked by the peon, "Why are you walking in as if this was your home?" Other surefire ways to get into officials' bad books are to fail to address them as Sir or Madam, to talk loudly or aggressively, and to rush them to do something when they are engaged in personal conversations.

A group which stands out within the category of the unknown client is the Burghers. This minority ethnic group remains alien to the lower and middle rungs of the administrative ladder, in dress (Western attire, especially among women), speech (English, though some Burghers speak Sinhala with a pronounced accent), and lighter complexion, as well as the shorter hair styles favored by the women. Once, when a Burgher entered the office, she was ignored by all of the clerks; when she finally attracted the attention of one of them -- a difficult task when no signs designate which clerk attends to which function -- she began to explain her case in English. The clerk looked on helplessly as the others in the office tried to suppress their laughter. Finally, AGA Douglas, who happened to be walking out of his office, came to her rescue. This highlights the fact that the average Sinhalese cannot empathize with the Burghers as they can with clients of the <u>ahimsaka</u> category. They retain none of the influence they had in colonial times,[1] and they have neither the political power nor the political connections to help them overcome the disadvantages of being unknown. The Burghers remain a relic of the colonial era.

The consensus of opinion about unknown clients varies between two extremes. Simon states that

> All kinds of people come and try to get things
> done through us: our friends, friends of our
> friends, and their friends. Then there are
> those who come to get things done forcibly.
> They all have one thing in common -- they want
> to complete their transaction as soon as
> possible.

To this Kamala adds, "And we try to meet their requests as soon as possible, too, so long as we are treated (salakannē) well by them." The term "treated" is a blanket expression which, while formally meaning to be polite and friendly, in this context could mean to be suitably recompensed, whether materially or otherwise.

On the other extreme is AGA Somapala, who says that:

> Our job is to be tactful and to keep our
> clients happy. All sorts of types come here.
> There are the loud talkers, aggressive ones
> and the passive ones. We must learn to handle
> them accordingly. If we shout at the
> aggresive type it won't work. Instead we must
> try to cool him down. Now this client: I

can't really help him with his rice ration
book. He has to go to the clerk first, but I
listened to his plea and then sent him to the
subject clerk. This pleases him. Even if you
cannot help you must show that you are trying
to help.

Clients Who Are Officials in Other Government Offices

Certain officials are definitely beyond the brother officer
category, but are linked in terms of the services they can
exchange. Thus, the regional manager of the Co-op Wholesale
Establishment (CWE) calls AGA Douglas and asks how he should go
about transferring his brother's ration book from Ganvälla to
Colombo. Douglas says, "Ah, that is a simple matter. You send
the book with a note and I will do it for you." The regional
manager has authority and control over food, clothing and
implements which are scarce, and over which the CWE has a
monopoly. By pleasing this client, the AGA does not expect
immediate reciprocity but insures himself for the future. The
same strategy is used when the assistant commissioner of
agrarian services brings an application to buy a tractor at the
subsidized rates given to cultivators, and when the local bank
manager requests a gun license.

The following case illustrates a different tactic on the
part of the AGA.

Case Eighteen. At the height of the cement shortage, two
clients who are employed by the CWE request a cement permit.
The AGA impresses on them that his stock is limited and that he
can therefore grant only emergency requests, for example for
funerals. One client replies, 'We need just two more bags to
finish cementing the floor of my kitchen before the new year.'
The AGA says, 'According to my list of permits issued and the
stock in hand, two clients who applied for permits and for whom

permits have been written have not come to pick these up yet.
So this stock should be in the co-op. If you hurry you might be
able to beat them to it.' Then he adds, 'How about bringing me
a couple of pounds of dried fish -- this is so hard to get these
days, especially with the scarcity of fresh fish.' One client
says, 'Of course, we can get you as many pounds as you want, and
we also have soap -- both washing and toilet, and also boxes of
matches.' The AGA replies, 'You better see about this first,'
handing him Rs. 10/., 'and we'll see about the rest later, if
you can come back with the dried fish around 12 p.m.' As the
clients leave he calls Karunapala, the subject clerk, and
authorizes him to write out a permit for them. The clients
return around noon, with some change and a couple of boxes of
matches, and say that they have left the fish in the AGA's car,
which is parked at the rear of the office building. The AGA
thanks them and hands them their permit, adding, 'Now you better
hurry to the co-op.'

In this case, the parties exchanged rare commodities to
which they have privileged access. Just as the AGA distributes
his limited supply of cement according to his own priorities, it
is a well-publicized fact that, although scarce goods sold in
the co-ops are theoretically available to all customers, in
practice such goods vanish from the counters as soon as they are
put out. They eventually find their way into the hands of the
friends of the co-op manager and employees. In this case,
unlike the one involving the regional manager, the reciprocal
transaction is completed at once. It is also interesting to
note that, while the AGA delayed a reciprocal request from the
regional manager of the CWE himself, he made an immediate
request of the two employees. It is likely that he could use
the regional manager for a bigger and better deal in the future.

A different type of transaction occurred between the
assistant commissioner of the Land Reform Commission (LRC) and
the AGA:

Case Nineteen. The AGA calls the assistant commissioner of
the LRC and says, 'First, I want to talk to you regarding that
baktigee [devotional songs] group of the YMBA [Young Men's
Buddhist Association, of which he is the president]. Can we get
them for our variety show on the 22nd of May [the Republic Day
celebrations]?' The LRC official replies, 'For that you have to
get the permission of the secretary of the National Association
in Colombo.' The AGA says, 'I don't want that group. I am
interested in that local group. Didn't you have a contest some
time ago and select the best local group? I was thinking of
them.' The assistant commissioner says, 'Yes, they are good.
It can be arranged, but you will have to give them transport.'
The AGA agrees and says, 'I will take care of that and I will
also see that this will get a lot of publicity and also make an
announcement that this singing was arranged by the chairman of
the YMBA.' The assistant commissioner concludes, 'Fine, then it
can be done.'

The AGA goes on to say, 'There is this other thing, Edwin.
There is this nephew of mine, my brother's son -- he sat for his
GCE [General Certificate of Education] and he has three passes.
He is English-speaking and he is a young fellow. Is there some
vacancy in the LRC janawasas [government colonization
projects]?' The assistant commissioner replies, 'Yes, you can
bring him over.' The AGA asks, 'Can you do this for me?' The
official replies, 'Yeah, it can be done. You bring him over on
Monday or Tuesday.'[2]

Like the transaction between the AGA and the CWE employees, this
was conducted and reciprocated here and now. But this case is
different as well. At first glance, it appears that the AGA is
making two requests of the LRC official: for the YMBA choir and
for a job for his nephew. But in fact, the AGA used the first
request to flatter the official, since asking for the choir's
services conferred an honor on the other man. He then drove
home his advantage by mentioning the publicity he would give to

the event and its organizers. In between, he get the promise of
what he really wanted: the job for his nephew.

   The following case illustrates a situation wherein the AGA
is initially reluctant to grant a request to an unknown client,
but changes his mind when he sees an advantage to doing so.

   Case Twenty. A man comes with a document and asks the AGA
to endorse it so that he can get his child's infant milk
permit. The AGA examines it and says, 'This is not a birth
certificate. You must bring the certificate, otherwise how can
I endorse this? This does not even have a name on it. What is
the child's name?' The client answers, 'It is written in this
letter which my GS gave me.' The AGA then says, 'You should get
the birth certificate of the child from the hospital and bring
it. I can't certify this.' The client replies, 'The secretary
and staff at the hospital are on strike; they won't do these
things now. I went and tried so many times and finally I came
to you today.' The AGA says 'I don't think the paramedical
staff are on strike.' The client, however, says that they are,
and so the AGA calls the hospital to check.

   The AGA speaks to the secretary, who confirms that there has
indeed been a strike, but that it has ended this morning. The
AGA says, 'Then if I send this person, he can get his
certificate either today or tomorrow, no? He can't get his milk
or food permit without that certificate.' The secretary -- whom
Douglas did not even know by name before making this call --
seizes this opportunity to ask a favor of the AGA; he asks for a
couple of bags of cement. The AGA says, 'The situation is bad
now. I only have a few left, for funerals, and that too is
dwindling fast. When I get the stocks I'll give you some
promptly; I'll give you a call and let you know.

   The AGA then says to the client, 'There, they have ended the
strike; now you can go and get it.' The client says, 'But there
must be a backlog of work there, and mine will get postponed
indefinitely.' Douglas gives him an intent look and says,

'Where do you work?' The client replies, 'At the People's
Bank.' The AGA is thoughtful for a moment, and then says, 'Oh,
this; I can deal with it myself. No need to have the birth
certificate.' He takes the letter from the GS to the client and
endorses it with his approval for an infant's milk permit. The
deciding factor was the fact that the client is employed by the
bank where the AGA has his account; since it is a well-known
principle that in social transactions in public offices in Sri
Lanka, it is useful to have a known face, Douglas changes his
mind and agrees to the client's request.

Professionals as Clients

The administrator's attitude towards professionals is an
extension of that just described. Doctors, and specialists in
particular, figure prominently in this category, as do lawyers.
Their transactions with the official are always speedy and
smooth. Very often they approach the AGA directly, though
occasionally they will go to a clerk if he or she is their
client. In either case they are known as "Attorney" or
"Doctor." The administrator assumes that, should the need
arise, he can rely on their services in the future.

Members of all ethnic groups belong to the professional
category. Lawyers are largely Sinhalese or Muslim, and a few
are Burghers; all are permanent residents of the community.
Doctors are primarily Tamils and Sinhalese, though a few are
Muslims and Burghers; some of the doctors are transient -- e.g.,
those attached to government hospitals -- and others, private
practitioners, are permanently settled. While there is a
certain overt familiarity underlying the relationship between
the official and the "other government empoyees," the
relationship between the administrator and the professional is
rather one of mutual and respectful cordiality.

Entrepreneurs as Clients

Merchants and small businessmen (<u>mudalālis</u>) are nearly
always noveau riche. They can manipulate administrators simply
because they make money. The consensus of opinion among the
officials is that the <u>mudalāli</u> is an unscrupulous shark, a black
marketeer who fleeces his poor customers. They think that even
the most (apparently) charitable act on the part of a <u>mudalāli</u>
has an ulterior motive. When a boat capsized on the river and a
number of people were drowned, a <u>mudalāli</u> volunteered the
coffins for those whose relatives lacked the means to supply
them. Most officials speculated that these coffins were made of
cheap wood, and that this was merely a publicity stunt to draw
attention to the merchant's wares, for he was indeed a dealer in
coffins.

Thus the administrator tries to get what he can from a
<u>mudalāli</u>. This manifests itself in different ways.

<u>Case Twenty-One</u>. A Muslim shopkeeper requests a permit for
barbed wire, saying that he needs to put a fence around his
garden. He speaks to the SA, whom he has known personally for
years, and the permit is granted immediately rather than after
the usual delay of a couple weeks. As he leaves, the SA says
that, for all he knows, the shopkeeper may sell the wire on the
black market. Having granted him this favor, however, the SA
knows that he could, for example, go to this man's shop and get
himself a good pair of leather shoes for below cost...and this
he did, only a week later.

Here is another case:

<u>Case Twenty-Two</u>. It is the practice of the Sri Lanka
government to draft private vehicles into service during times
of emergency. During the 1971 insurrection, such vehicles were
used by the armed forces. Privately owned vehicles may also be

used by cooperatives when they are short of the vehicles needed to transport food supplies from warehouses to the local co-ops.

A smiling male client walks up to AGA Somapala, who says pleasantly, 'Why, I approved your gun permit; didn't you get it yet?' The client says that he did receive it, and that his visit is about another matter entirely. Seeing me, however, he is reluctant to state his case until the AGA explains to him the reason for my presence. Reassured, the client explains, 'I came regarding that lorry belonging to my father which you have drafted for co-op work. We have a problem; that particular lorry is out of action, otherwise we would have certainly obliged you, and at the moment our other lorries are busy in our regular business. This is a particularly busy season transporting paddy from the fields to the government stores,' a function which is indeed privately contracted. 'Otherwise we would have given you one of the other vehicles.' The AGA says, 'It's okay, we will find another vehicle.'

As the client leaves, Piyadasa tells me, 'Have you seen his bakery and tea room? It is located at a very good spot. If you are nice to the man, we can at least go in and have a [free] cup of tea on our way to the office and back.'

Here is a third example of official-entrepreneur interaction.

Case Twenty-Three. Alfred, the 'godfather' of entrepreneurs, is perhaps the case par excellence to illustrate the bureaucrac-entrepreneur relationship. He rose from rags to riches and today owns a chain of shops, houses, and estates. His main interest continues to be his electrical appliance shop, which is the nucleus of his business interests. His manipulatory strength lies solely in his business supplies and financial resources while socially, he enjoys almost no esteem. To his face he is addressed as Alfred mudalāli, but behind his back officials refer disdainfully to his humble origins.

Alfred's liking for hard liquor is well known. On any evening he can be seen at either the Rest House or the Public Services Club, the popular gathering places for the local elite; Alfred spends hundreds of rupees on scotch for himself and anyone who cares to join him. He attracts the middle-level officers of the administration, and is often heard to brag that 'I know Mr. X, the Assistant Commissioner of Social Services. He is a good friend of mine. He had a drink with me last evening at the Rest House.' In a direct sense this obligates Mr. X to Alfred, such that he would have to use his influence to help Alfred in any transaction he may undertake. Still, Mr. X will also openly admit that he only keeps company with Alfred for the sake of the luxury liquor, since the social galas sponsored by the local administrative and service elite seldom include Alfred. His infrequent invitations to such events are usually a result of his donating a large sum of money to the cause in question, and even then, it is he alone, and not his family, who is invited.

Other than treating officers to food and drink and contributing lavishly to their pet schemes, Alfred uses another tactic which is widely employed by entrepreneurs. If a customer who is an official comes to Alfred's appliance store, Alfred will instruct his assistant to give the man a considerable discount. This has come to be expected over the years, and Alfred indeed says, 'If I send my assistant and instruct him to say that this request is from the Ganvälla Appliance Shop, they immediately know that by being cooperative, they will certainly get treated well by me in the future.' His customary practice is to send an assistant bearing his request, and at times the assistants made requests of their own as well, but in either case the request is phrased as being from the Ganvälla Appliance Shop. Thus on different occasions, Alfred's assistants have visited the AGA's office to ask for ration books, gun licenses, and cartridge permits, all of which they received.

Transaction through the "Gift"

Finally, the traditional Sinhalese practice of gift giving in the case of the normal unknown, and even in certain instances the "aggressive unknown," facilitates interactions with the official. The clients get what they want without undue delay, and without the inconvenience and expense of frequent visits.

One might ask whether such gifts are truly gifts, in the traditional sense, or whether they constitute bribes. Spiro (1962), Leys (1965), Wertheim (1965), Taub (1969), and Price (1975) argue that the gift in traditional societies easily shades into corruption. This may well be the case in Sri Lanka as well; still, this is not necessarily a modern trend. It could be maintained (Pieris 1956:118) that the traditional institution of the gift always contained the potential for being abused.

There are, however, differences between the traditional gift and its modern incarnation. In a patrimonial bureaucracy, officials did not receive fixed salaries in cash. Instead, the gift was the conventional method of payment; not being fixed in amount, there was room for extortion. In the modern rational bureaucracy, officials are paid fixed, cash salaries and the gift is felt to be neither proper nor necessary. It is not a part of the institutional-official complex. But at the behavioral level, it continues to be used by those officials and clients who think they can benefit from it. To this category belong officials at the bottom of the salary scale and those clients who have no other method of getting what they want from the bureaucracy.

In the AGA's office, one of the minor employees constantly solicited gifts. Sometimes he accepted cash, ranging from Rs. 2/. for obtaining a permit to Rs. 20/. for pilfering coupons from rice ration books. A dram of arrack, a local liquor, was the next in value, and lesser items included cigarettes and cups of tea. A clerk was alleged to accept gifts of the same kind.

Case Twenty-Four. A man -- old, toothless, bespectacled and
wearing trousers rather than a cloth or sarong -- comes to the
AGA's office and walks past the SA toward Kamala's desk. Seeing
that it is vacant, he walks back to the SA and says, 'It is
about a timber permit.' The SA tells him that Kamala is not in
today, and the client replies, 'I am here on behalf of my son,
who said that he entrusted the job -- vādē bāra dunna -- to a
person called Jamis.' The SA says, 'Yes, he is there,'
pointing, 'inside that room.' The client goes in, returning to
the main office with Jamis. The latter sorts through the files
on Kamala's desk and hands a document to the client, saying,
'This is your permit.' The client takes it and walks away; but,
having reached the verandah, he pauses and signals Jamis to join
him. The latter walks toward the client and says, 'Do you have
the Rs. 10/.?' The client hands him the money.

Others like Simon and Kamala, who criticized Pediric and
Jamis for such practices, were not averse to receiving gifts on
occasion. As earlier described, they employed sarcasm and broad
hints to convince a client to bring them tea and biscuits.
Kamala once demanded a bunch of king coconuts -- a beverage
fruit which is increasingly difficult to buy, a single fruit
costing as much as Rs. 1/. -- for swift handling of a timber
permit. While accepting the permit application, she remarked
loudly how difficult and expensive these fruits have become, and
the client offered to bring her some. She publicly refused the
offer, but two days later the client reappeared with a bunch of
about 20 king coconuts, which Kamala stored in the back room
until it was time to go home.

When officials are discussing the gift in formal
conversations, those among them who accept it refer to it not as
allasa [bribe, the term used by their critics[3]], but as tāgga
[gift], santōsama [expression of happiness], daṅduvama [penalty,
presumably for the client], or ganu dēnu [give-take]. Some may
simply ask a client, 'What will you give us?' There is a moral

hierarchy of gift practices, some being more reprehensible than
others. While Jamis extorted gifts of all types, he was most
heavily criticized by the others (including Simon and Kamala)
for demanding money from clients. As in the case of the
traditional gift, its contemporary counterpart is given after
the fact; the client knows that if he reneges, he forfeits all
hope of receiving favors in the future.

Transactions through Coercion: Verbal Persuasion

Officials, like anyone else, like to maintain a positive
relationship with the police. The official can then expect
protective intervention from the police, both for himself and
for others who may find themselves on the wrong side of the law.

Case Twenty-Five. A police inspector, Randeniya, comes to
the AGA with a companion. Without much ado, Randeniya says, 'I
want five bags of cement.' AGA Douglas replies, 'Well, to tell
you the plain truth, I have cement only for funerals.' After
reading over the application, he says, 'This is for 25 bags,
no? It's impossible.' The inspector smiles, but says in a
subtly threatening tone, 'Is that so? This is for the Ganvälla
devale [temple]. He wants to complete repairs to that building
before the festival.'
The festival to which he refers is a major religious event
in Sri Lanka, and its organization and sponsorship have become
political events. Both the local MP, a member of the opposition
group in parliament, and the government party organizer have
been using the festival to court popularity on the eve of the
general elections. While the AGA's political sympathies are
with the MP, he privately detests the party organizer for his
use of thuggery and violence. The inspector's companion is a
well-known ally of the party organizer. Douglas thus replies,
'That is impossible. We have got only 150 bags. Out of this we
set aside 40 for election purposes,' referring to the repair of

roads to polling booths, the construction of restrooms, and the
provision of other amenities for officials on election duty.
'The rest is for funerals and even then I'm giving only two per
permit. The request for funerals is unlike that for any other
reason. It is terrible if you cannot bury a man because of the
lack of cement.'

The inspector then inquires why lavatories must be built for
those engaged in election work: 'Why can't they make temporary
cadjan huts?' referring to coconut palm huts. Douglas shrugs
his shoulders and says, 'Don't know.' The inspector continues,
'People must be lying and requesting cement for funerals.'
Douglas replies, 'I don't know. It seems that these days a lot
of people have died.' He takes out his register to prove this
point, showing them that he had issued nine permits already that
day just for funerals. The inspector then says, 'Nowhere else
in the country do people use all this cement to bury the dead.
Now in the Kandyan districts...' Douglas says, 'But this is the
way it is done here. People feel that they must do their best
for the dead as last respects.'[4]

AGA Douglas then turns to Randeniya's companion and says,
'You better put this off 'til a later date,' but the client says
that he wants to finish the work before the festival: 'Can't
you give me at least 10 bags?' Both clients resolutely stand
their ground, and Douglas finally capitulates, saying, 'You
know, if you don't feel any compunction about taking away
someone's funeral quota I will give you two bags and state that
it is for a funeral, and I am doing this for his sake,' with a
frustrated look indicating the inspector. Randeniya's ally
replies, 'What can I do with two bags? Can you give me at least
five?' Douglas says, 'Can't do that.'

The clients continue to employ the standard strategy of
persistence, waiting silently and refusing to acknowledge the
AGA's refusal. By staying they hope to reverse his decision,
and 10 minutes later, after Douglas has dealt with another
client, he comes back to them and says, 'I will make out two

permits for cement for funerals, under both your names, and give
two bags per permit. Then you will get four bags.' The
inspector's ally says, 'Why can't you make it five?' Douglas,
visibly annoyed, replies, 'If I give you a permit for five bags
for funerals, someone else can quote your case and ask for the
same. These permits go to the co-op, and the people there will
wonder why.' The inspector's companion then says, 'Then I will
write out two letters of request for permits, stating that they
are for two funerals in Ganwalla.' The inspector tells him
'Yes, you do that,' and leaves.

At this point, Douglas stares at the client with unconcealed
hostility, angry at having been coerced into a decision contrary
to his convictions, and says, 'Now if I give you this cement,
people will say that I did it out of fear of the police.' He is
aware that the co-op employees will know of this transaction,
and, recognizing his name, spread the word through the
community. But the client says, his facial expression betraying
his words, 'Not through fear but for friends.' AGA Douglas
replies, 'How can I give it to you when I have refused my
brother officers? Only this morning the Additional GA wanted
cement and I explained my position to him. If I were you I
would drop this whole matter, This is election time. This is
not the right time to do these things. This is all a political
tactic on your part and that of the party organizer. One can
never say what might happen after the elections. Surely you
have sense to see whether building something in the devale is
more important than giving cement to build a grave.' He looks
expectantly at the client, but the latter, though looking
sheepish, adamantly refuses to relent. The AGA is thus finally
forced to authorize a permit for four bags of cement, ostensibly
for a funeral.

Transactions through Coercion: Physical Force

The threat is much more explicit in the case of transactions between the official and the local kalu haraka [black bull]. Originally a fish vendor at the public market, this man was edged out by a gang more ferocious than his. He then sold beef at the bus stop and, along with the color of his skin, this earned him the nickname of kalu haraka. From beef he moved on to illicit liquor and drugs, which he sells at his shack by the bridge.

The kalu haraka strong-arms the rich. His latest scheme was taking up a donation of electric light bulbs, ostensibly to light up the bodhi [sacred bo tree and its temple]; having collected about 250 bulbs, he sold them and kept the profits. He has also gathered a gang of unemployed urban youth who, under his direction, pick pockets around the bus stop. The black bull's innumerable altercations with the police have at times earned him rough treatment at their hands. The following is an account of one of his visits to the office:

Case Twenty-Six. A dark, thick-set man in his mid-thirties, wearing an unbuttoned nylon shirt and a short sarong, staggers into the office followed by a male companion. His attire is that of the typical hoodlum in Sri Lanka, and he has obviously been drinking heavily. He stops at the SA's desk and, nearly incoherently, demands a valuation certificate, which is a document given by the AGA's office, once the client has produced a property deed, to certify the property's value. Valuation certificates are required by the courts as bond for bailing out offenders.

The SA tells the man that the AGA is on leave, and that Ranasinghe, the headquarters AGA, is acting in his place. He also says, however, that Ranasinghe is in the kachcheri and has not yet come to the AGA's office. He suggests that the client go to the kachcheri and meet with him there; he has to repeat

the name and title of the official for the client, who finally
leaves to seek out Ranasinghe. After the two men leave, a hush
falls over the office; Chandra and Rosilin look stricken.
Finally Simon whispers, 'Do you know who that was?' and Chandra
replies, 'He is the one who insulted my uncle the other day, in
my presence.'

Five minutes later the client returns, saying that though
Ranasinghe's car was parked outside the kachcheri, he had not
been in the office. The SA says that, since the car is there,
Ranasinghe is sure to show up at some time. The black bull
then returns to the kachcheri with his companion. Only minutes
later they return with the official, who walks into the AGA's
room, orders tea for himself, and makes a phone call. After
this the two men present their case to him. The SA gives the
kalu haraka's documents to Chandra, the subject clerk, and asks
her to see that they are in order. She is tense, and her hands
are shaking. After a cursory glance at the documents, she says
that they are in order and begins to write out the valuation
certificate, which must be completed in triplicate.

Midway through this task, Chandra notices that the client
has not paid his dues to the office for this certificate.
Meanwhile, the black bull comes in from the verandah and sits
down in the chair opposite from Chandra and the SA. He crosses
his legs and nonchalantly takes out a pack of cigarettes and
lights one-- a sign of defiance in the presence of elders or
authority figures. He then offers one to his companion, who is
still on the verandah, but the latter seems reluctant to smoke
in the office. The kalu haraka then throws the pack at him, but
he gives it back, still refusing to smoke.

Meanwhile, the black bull has put his feet up on a chair,
another sign of defiance, and has been watching Chandra intently
as she works. She asks the SA to write out a receipt for a deed
valued at Rs. 3000/., i.e., Rs. 30/. The black bull calls in
his companion and says, 'Ah, pay up, pay up.' The latter pays
and gets his receipt, and Chandra goes on filling out the form.

The black bull restlessly shuffles his feet until Simon comes
in and greets him; he offers him a cigarette too, but Simon says
he can't smoke in the office. Simon then notices that the black
bull has a scar about 10 inches long on his right arm, and asks
how he got it. The kalu haraka says, 'Oh, in a small fight the
other day. You know, I always carry this kris knife here,'
indicating the waist of his sarong, where a knife handle is
partly visible. 'Premadasa tried to jokingly take it away from
me and I pulled it back, in the course of which I was
accidentally cut.'

Simon had earlier been bragging about his acquaintance with
the black bull , while the latter was off looking for
Ranasinghe; he claimed to have hidden a member of his gang from
the police. Chandra had said that Simon should stay in the
office so that he could tell his acquaintance what he needed to
be told when he returned. Now, as Chandra continues filling out
the document, Simon says to the kalu haraka, 'These things take
time to write; she will be through soon.' But the black bull
walks over to Chandra's desk, staring intently at her hand and
noticing its unsteadiness; he grins sardonically and says, 'A
nona nona [Lady, hurry].' He then taunts her, saying, 'I can do
this quicker.' Chandra looks panicked, as do the other
officials. Finally, 15 minutes after she began writing, the
document is ready, and Simon takes it to Ranasinghe for his
signature. The latter is on the phone, but the black bull
interrupts him and demands that he sign it quickly. Ranasinghe
signs the document, and Simon brings it back to Chandra. The
kalu haraka tries to take it from him, saying, 'Now, do I take
all of these documents?' Simon answers, 'No, you keep these and
we keep these,' smiling, 'you don't know these things because
someone has been doing it for you all the while.' The black
bull nods his head in agreement and leaves.

There is a sigh of relief throughout the office, though
Chandra is still noticeably shaken. For the next few minutes,
the SA, Chandra, Simon, and Rosilin discuss the black bull --

the details of his atrocities and his police record. A week
later, he returns on another errand, which is transacted equally
smoothly. On this occasion, AGA Somapala is present and asks if
I know who this man is. I say that I do, and he says, 'You have
to be careful with such people; handle them tactfully.'

Like the police officer in the earlier case, the kalu haraka
manages to negotiate a nearly impossible transaction in record
time. Most unknown clients would not have been able to get this
done in the absence of the AGA, for the official who acts in the
AGA's stead makes an appearance only in absolute emergencies.[5]

The Political Monk[6]

Besides the members of aristocratic families, in traditional
Sinhalese society there are three social roles which are
accorded high prestige. The occupants of these roles have
traditionally been regarded as popular leaders and molders of
public opinion. These are Buddhist monks, school teachers, and
practitioners of indigenous medicine: sanga, guru, and veda,
respectively.

In today's semi-urban setting of the bureaucracy, neither
the school teacher nor the ayurvedic physician possesses much
manipulatory power, though should a guru or veda belong to one
of the categories of the known face, he qualifies for
preferential treatment. But unlike the traditional elite, whose
social position engenders positive attitudes in the official,
and unlike the teacher or physician who may qualify as "known,"
the monk who has become worldly cannot hope to find favor in the
eyes of the official.

The official makes a distinction between the robe and its
wearer. For example, a Buddhist monk requests the creation of a
new grama sevaka division for the village where his temple and
school are located. AGA Sompala makes preliminary inquiries,

and when the monk arrives to find out the results, he is
received with due respect: the AGA stands up, offers the monk a
seat, and addresses him as <u>swāmīn</u> <u>vahansē</u> [reverend]. However,
he tells the monk that his appeal must be rejected because the
area in question is too small: it encompasses only three-
quarters of a mile and, since it has 2,000 rice ration books, it
has only 2,000 residents while a new GS division must have at
least 5,000 rice ration books. The monk leaves, saying "I will
somehow get this done." The AGA tells me, "That priest is doing
all kinds of unnecessary things. Not at all like a Buddhist
priest. He is an insult to the robe. He surrounds himself with
young females. The other day, the GA asked him, 'Reverend, why
are you surrounding yourself with dancing females? [<u>mokada</u>
<u>hāmudurvane</u> <u>gānu</u> <u>lamayi</u> <u>tiyāgena</u> <u>natavannē</u>]]' and the priest
replied, 'Sir, I like to do artistic things [<u>mama</u> <u>kalā</u> <u>deval</u>
<u>karanna</u> <u>āsayi</u>].'"

On another occasion, reverend Jinendrawanda comes to the
AGA's office and, walking into the AGA's room, finds that it is
vacant. He then comes back to the main office and tries to get
someone's attention. Ordinarily, one would expect the official
to set aside his immediate task to draw up a chair for the
priest and inquire as to the reason for his visit. However, on
this occasion the monk paces about for five minutes before the
SA inquires, in much the same way he would ask a lay client, why
the monk has come to the office. The priest requests a cement
permit and the SA tells him that this subject is now handled
directly by the AGA, who is absent for the day. The monk is
told to come back at a later date and, as he leaves, the SA
says, "These priests are too much. Covered in yellow, they
think that they can come and do what they want. Why would he
need cement anyway? It is these <u>upāsaka</u> <u>ammās</u> [pious lay women]
who spoil them -- they feed them, fall at their feet and worship
them!"

Another example of the treatment accorded the political monk
is reverend Mahinda's request for a plot of land under the

government's middle-class land alienation scheme. This is
rejected by AGA Douglas, who tells him, "You don't belong to any
class. The middle class by definition are those who are in the
Rs. 15,000 - 20,000 income group. You say that you have only an
income of Rs. 150/. and that too is not yours. It is given by
your dāyakayās [donors]." The AGA crosses out the application
and throws it in the trash, then tells me, in an outraged tone,
that the monk is trying to obtain the land for his kinsman.

Finally, in discussing the problems faced by farmers in the
village of Ganegoda, the agricultural officer says,

> The fields here are very fertile, but the
> yield is always low. The farmers are
> unwilling to mature the fields, because with
> the slightest rain this area is subject to
> floods. When this happens the manure and the
> seedlings just float in the water and get
> washed away. The floods could be controlled
> if the mouth of the anicut which feeds these
> fields is widened to allow the flood waters to
> pass. But there are temple buildings right
> next to the land and it will mean that they
> will have to be demolished. Given that the
> chief priest is a strong ally of the local MP,
> this will never happen. There is another
> possibility -- another anicut could be built
> to divert the water from flowing north, but
> this will mean the flooding of certain
> adjacent fields which belong to the relatives
> of the same priest. He is a kerunkārayā
> [influential man], so nothing can be done to
> help out the poor farmers.

The attitude of the official to the political monk is one of
hostility due to the monk's failure (in the eyes of the
official) to live up to his vows of piety, poverty and charity.
This type of Buddhist monk has lost his traditional high status

and respect, but he is still a powerful factor in marshalling support for or against an individual by using religion as a rallying cry on the public platform. This has become a rich source of support for parliamentary politicians and the monks, in turn, have used this strength vis-à-vis the politicians to advance their own material ends and those of their kinsmen. Such use of the robe is condemned by the officials.

The MP's Letter

MPs write letters specifically requesting administrators to comply with their requests on behalf of a client who is generally a loyal supporter. Such a letter constitutes an order rather than a request. It demands that the official -- usually at least of the rank of AGA -- comply with the request.

The letter has both positive and negative aspects in client-official relationships. On the positive side, it is a resource in the hands of a client who has no other way of breaking through the formal facade of the bureaucracy in order to redress legitimate grievances. However, in the hands of the same client it could become a weapon to force the official to act contrary to every rule in the book for the client's selfish interests. Despite officials' resentment towards the client who negotiates a transaction through the use of the MP's letter, in eight out of ten cases requests set forth in letters are granted. As in the case of the worldly monk, the client who has recourse to the MP's letter underlies his request with a threat of possible punitive action. Such action often takes the form of a punishment transfer of the official, who may be posted to a remote administrative location.

Several types of unknown clients make use of the MP's letter. Some clients may request a plot of government land, and others may request compensation for damage caused by flood or fire. In both cases the letter will typically follow this format: "X is personally known to me. He is a poor man who has

.... Please give him...." Letters also arrive pleading the
case of such traditional figures as Buddhist priests, school
teachers, and practitioners of indigenous medicine. Prestigious
persons in the modern sense are also represented: members of
the youth league of the political party to which the MP belongs;
members of rural development societies; members of cultivation
committees who represent farmers' interests; and members of
agricultural productivity committees, whose task is to increase
food productivity by supplying seeds and tools, maintaining
canals and so on. Others include members of _janata_ committees,
the people's groups which monitor the activities of officials in
the government and in co-op enterprises; and members of the
board of directors of the Multi-purpose Co-op Service (MPCS),
the central coordinating body of the regional co-op stores.

The MP's letter may be used to request such things as timber
transport permits, liquor licenses, cement permits, and
government land. Because of the resentment of the MP's
interference in a sphere of authority which the AGA considers
his own, AGA Somapala often says angrily to a client, "Must you
bring the MP's letter for even this?" Still, he grants such
requests immediately, and gives priority to such cases when
disbursing scarce commodities such as land and social welfare
payments.

The Petition and the Unknown Client

In the hands of an "unknown helpless" client, the petition
is an instrument which reinforces the self-esteem and social
prestige of certain officials, notably the AGA and Additional
GA. In the hands of the unknown client, however, the petition
becomes a weapon which directly challenges the authority of
another category of officials, the _grama_ _sevakas_. Through this,
it also challenges the self-respect of the AGA and the
Additional GA. The petition as used by the unknown is not a
request for goods or services as in the case of the unknown

helpless; instead, it is a document of complaint against a minor
official such as a GS, or against a fellow client who is a
member of the community. Of these, petitions against the GS are
by far the most common. Complaints by members of the community
against each other are more likely to be settled through
alternative channels such as political pressure, police
authority, and conciliation boards.

The AGA says of such petitions,

> These petitions are a useless waste of time.
> They want someone to listen to their stories
> and they come here and waste my time.
> Sometimes I get angry and even scold them.
> Most of the allegations are minor and of a
> personal nature. The GS have a lot of work to
> do and they can't please everyone, and at
> times there is some truth in the allegations.
> But, one has to think of the grama sevaka's
> position. As a person from outside the area,
> he faces the opposition of people who are kin
> and friends. They obstruct his duties, send
> a petition and then don't turn up to give
> evidence.

The SA, on the other hand, says,

> Most of these grama sevakas are very corrupt.
> They always expect something, not necessarily
> money but even a pack of cigarettes. So when
> poor people go to the GS they find it
> difficult to get things done. On the other
> hand, these people also at times expect the GS
> to give false reports.[7] If the GS refuses,
> then the client will send a petition. The GS
> has a lot of work. He works most of the time
> [technically, he is on 24-hour duty six days a
> week] and this can be very frustrating. So he

takes it out on the people and the latter
complain through petitions.

Once a petition is sent, it usually takes the following
course: The AGA informs the accused and the victim that they
must come to his office at an appointed date and time for a
preliminary inquiry. Each party is also asked to bring
witnesses and objects or items which may be used as evidence.
At the end of this hearing, the AGA can dismiss the case and
simply issue a warning to the offender. If he feels there is a
legitimate case, however, the AGA informs the Additional GA, who
then conducts the next stage of the inquiry.

A perusal of more than 100 petitions which had accumulated
over a 10-year period, and attendance at a few hearings as well,
led to the following observations. There was one complaint made
by a client against the clerk who handles rice ration books, in
which the clerk was accused of discrimination. The client's
complaint was that he had arrived at the office before another
client who was acquainted with the clerk, and, being considered
"of no consequence," had been ignored -- tuttuwakatawat ganan
gattē nā.

There were also about 20 cases wherein clients complained
about other clients and in which the AGA was asked to
arbitrate. The majority of such petitions dealt with land
disputes, either boundary disputes involving alleged
encroachment, or usurping of rights in cases of joint
ownership. There were also petitions relating to domestic
disputes, frequently involving a wife accusing her husband of
physical cruelty or infidelity. Petitions among clients also
used the AGA as an instrument of maintaining morality in the
community, to curb such immoral behavior as adultery and, in one
case, father-daughter incest.

The majority of the petitions, however, were by a client or
a group of clients against a GS and another client or group in
the same GS division. The subjects of such petitions varied,
from complaints that the GS did not perform his duties well or

was never in his office -- the most common -- to allegations
that the poor cannot get things done or that the GS requests
bribes. Some grama sevakas were accused of being politically
partisan, of being drunkards, or of ignoring immoral activity,
as in the following petition:

> Since his arrival, about 20 illicit liquor-
> brewing centers have sprung up in the village.
> The GS gets 20 percent of the profits from
> this. When the excise officials plan a raid,
> the GS informs the offenders in advance, so
> that they go under cover. He keeps company
> with rabble rousers. The GS lives in a house
> belonging to Davith and is therefore partisan
> to the latter's wishes. He used his official
> position to harass Davith's opponents...[he]
> acts in his official capacity according to
> the latter's whims and fancies. Though the
> GS does not reside in this place now, yet if
> any complaint is made by us he always consults
> Davith before taking action. Because of this
> Davith and his brother Dasa Singho terrorize
> the village. The GS does not check them and
> he also prevents the police from taking
> action. As a result Davith and his brother
> have divided the village into two factions and
> those who are against them cannot get any
> services performed on their behalf by this GS.
> The other day Davith and his brother
> threatened to kill all -- and this is the GS's
> fault. The GS is prone to immoral behavior.
> The GS used obscene language when two young
> girls had gone to get character certificates
> from him. He told them, 'crazy nuisance;
> better if you came after 9 p.m.'

Another example of complaints involving a grama sevaka is taken from a petition alleging that the GS of Dangedera is never in his office; insults clients who come seeking his advice; seduced or raped a mute girl in the village; misbehaves at night, and with young women who visit his office for legitimate purposes; exploits women clients; and obstructs the devotees who visit the temple during poya days [Buddhist holy days].

In this instance, the AGA summoned the petitioner, the GS, and the witnesses for an inquiry. An examination of the GS's diary showed that, in regard to the first allegation, the petitioner had visited the GS's office on a Division Day, when the GS had to be at the AGA's office. The client had also come by on a day when the GS was at the kachcheri for a class.[8] Both of these excuses for his absence are quite legitimate since they are part of his official duties. The charge of insulting the client involved the following statements by the GS: taman dänaganna epäyä daruvō hadanna [one should know how to bring up one's own children better]; dat väti tiyennē niyangetayi [you have lost your teeth due to the drought and not to old age (this implying that the client, although elderly, is not worthy of respect)]; kata hoṅdayi bulat kotanna [your mouth is good for pounding betel (this being a disrespectful form of address)]. The AGA's interpretation is that these statements do not constitute insults.

As to the accusation of raping the mute girl, the girl's mother gives evidence that her daughter has never visited the GS unchaperoned. Since her son, however, is angry at the GS, he has spread this rumor of rape through an anonymous pamphlet, which the GS himself has seen. As to the charge of misbehaving at night, the GS affirms that his travels throughout the division after dark are simply to stop the illicit felling of timber (of which some of the petitioners themselves are guilty). The GS denies the accusations that he misbehaves with or exploits female clients, pointing out that his office is located in his house, where he lives with his wife, his mother, and several other persons. Since the clients conduct their dealings with him in public, as it were, there can be no opportunity for misbehavior.

Regarding the final charge, of insulting the devotees of the local temple, the AGA hears evidence from the chief monk of that temple, a respected member of the community. The monk testifies that, to his knowledge, the GS has not insulted the worshippers or used obscene language. He also states that the GS is a pious man who frequents the temple to pay obesiance, who helps with temple activities on pōya days, and who neither misbehaves nor gets drunk.

After hearing the evidence, the AGA concludes that the petition was instigated by those clients who were apprehended by the GS for illicit timber felling and liquor brewing. These people have created a faction in the village and seen to it that the petition was submitted. The petition is dismissed, but the petitioners use their influence with the MP to have the GS transferred to another division. The Grama Sevaka Association in turn protests that there is no place for an honest and efficient official.

The frustration that a grama sevaka can experience, as well as the damage to his self-esteem and social prestige, is revealed in a petition of appeal a GS submitted to his superior, the AGA:

> The high priest of Veragala temple sent his
> driver and asked me for a letter to get a
> cement permit. I said that I cannot give the
> letter like that, that he must first bring a
> letter explaining the reason for the request.
> And he left. The next morning I toured my
> division in the company of another official.
> We saw the priest, who talked to us and said,
> Why didn't tamusē [a derogatory way of saying
> "you"] give cement? Are you against us? I
> told the GA and he gave me a permit for 150

bags. There we even brought them home. They
treat us well, unlike you petty officials.' I
tried to explain the rules pertaining to
obtaining a cement permit, and the priest,
without listening to me, insulted me. I had
to face this situation because of the
privileges given to the priest by the GA. In
a situation like this I felt ashamed. This is
detrimental to your self-image (pradēspayē api
räkagena yana garutvaya paludu vīmata ida
äta). Therefore, taking necessary action is
your responsibility.

Signed,

GS_____

The grama sevaka feels let down by his superior, the GA, and
appeals for the protection of his immediate superior, the AGA.
The latter is unable to do much in the face of the GA's action.
He sends a letter to the monk explaining the formal procedure
followed in issuing cement permits, thereby hoping to exonerate
the GS. One supposes that the GS was himself pressured into
giving away the cement by a politician supporting the monk.

Inquiry into a Petition:
A Female Client's Complaint against the GS

The client in question says that she caught a 6:30 p.m. bus
at the Gamwalla bus stop. The AGA asks whether she has the
ticket stub as proof that she traveled on that bus, but she says
that she did not keep it. The AGA says that, in that case,
there is no proof. She continues, "I was seated in the back of
the bus, and the GS was outside. He said to me, Is it bad for
you to come to my house, you patta vēsi [bloody whore]?' He
insulted me before a crowd of strangers."

The AGA then asks why she did not complain to the security officials at the bus stop, but she says that she was fearful of provoking the GS, who was under the influence of liquor. The AGA asks how she could know this, since she was on the bus and he was outside; she replies, "I thought so because he scolded me in a filthy manner." The AGA points out that everyone who speaks in such a manner is not drunk, but the client says that others who witnessed the incident said that he was drunk. The AGA says, "How do you know? You just thought so. It is a matter of opinion," and then asks if she knows why the GS should be antagonistic towards her. The client says that she has never even spoken to him before, that he is not even the official who has jurisdiction over her area.

She goes on to conjecture that his behavior was because "I have some relatives residing in his division who are angry with me over a property dispute, and the GS is very friendly with them. He always visits them and uses their well." The AGA says that he cannot take action since she has no witnesses or proof of the incident: "I have to conclude that you have fabricated this story because of private vengeance toward this GS. You should have asked the conductor of the bus to protect you, or else gone to the police station." The client says that the others on the bus counseled her to keep quiet (pāduvē inna), "but the thing is that he insulted me in the bazaar, and I can't show my face."

The AGA finally says, "You should have at least taken your umbrella and hammered him. Then there would be a case to take to the police, and there would be evidence. Now if I take any action without evidence, this GS could take either political or administrative action against me." The client leaves, promising to bring witnesses to the next hearing. The following day she returns, accompanied by a man. The AGA is absent, however, away on election work. After waiting around for a while, the client leaves and this petition is not heard again.

In contrast, definite action was taken in each of the
following three cases.

Case Twenty-Seven. A series of complaints against the GS of
Kotugodella results in his transfer. According to the AGA, 'He
uses bad language on clients even in my presence. Therefore I
can well believe the complaints against him. He may be an
efficient official in that he conforms to rules and
regulations. But first and foremost he should be a good human
being. It cannot be said that vices increased because of him.
The GS alone is unable to check all illegal activities; he
should receive police assistance. Nevertheless, there are
constant petitions against the GS. It shows that he is unable
to perform his duties with public good will. There is a section
of the population against him. This is not because he did not
do his duty as a GS, but because he did not know how to speak to
his clients. Therefore, he should be transferred -- for his own
well-being and that of his clients.'

Case Twenty-Eight. The GS of Naimada is dismissed for
misappropriating cash and foodstuffs left in his charge for
flood relief victims. The latter complain to the AGA, saying
that they can prove, with facts and figures, how this GS
distributed the supplies in his own area: he gave them to his
cronies, who were in fact not affected by the floods. Also, he
is accused of using the names of certain victims and claiming
the compensation due to them, for himself. After the AGA's
inquiry, a second inquiry is undertaken by the Additional GA, on
whose advice the GA dismisses the GS from service. The GS
appeals to the Public Service Commission to have mercy on him,
on the grounds that he is a family man with five children and
elderly parents who are also dependent on him. But his appeal
is dismissed.

Case Twenty-Nine. An accusation is brought against a GS by
an assistant secretary to the Minister of Defense. Private land
belonging to her is in the process of being acquired by the
government under the Land Reform Act. Until the legalities are
completed, the land is still technically the secretary's
property. During this time, however, the GS and his friends
plucked 200 coconuts from trees on the property and were caught
in the act. The secretary submits a petition against the GS,
who pleads guilty on the grounds that he was under the
impression that the government had already acquired the land.
After an inquiry, the GS is found guilty, his increments are
suspended, and he is required to reimburse the petitioner the
cost of the 200 coconuts.

The subjects of petitions range widely, from vague
accusations of neglect of duty to complaints of personal abuse,
and the conduct of inquiries into petitions is equally varied.
Some begin with a formal preliminary inquiry involving the
accused, the victim, and witnesses, and move on to a second
inquiry; others result in dismissal after the preliminary
inquiry. At times, no inquiry is held, but a simple letter of
reprimand is issued instead. There is a direct correlation
between the nature of the allegation and the speed with which
the inquiry is held and the decision made. But the majority of
petitions are merely what the AGA termed "useless and a waste of
time," involving not such weighty matters as embezzlement but
simple abuse and insult. These petitions seldom warrant a
systematic inquiry.

Complaints are occasionally lodged with the local MP and the
Minister of Public Administration. This is reflected in the
following circular, sent to the kachcheri and the AGA by the
secretary to the minister:

>   It is sad to hear that most grama sevakas do
>   not perform their duties satisfactorily.
>   While allegations against them are increasing,

the people think that we don't take any action
and thus they have criticized the government.
I ask on behalf of the minister, to inquire
promptly into all allegations and not feel
sorry for the offender. All GS should be
exemplary government servants -- anyone who
cannot maintain this standard need not be in
service. Therefore quick action against them
should be taken by the AGA.

Petitions, the Petitioned, and the Petitioner

This section outlines conclusions emerging from the
treatment of the petition in which the GS was accused of abuse.
Since the charges do not involve violations of financial or
other codes, the AGA, who makes the formal inquiry, either
treats them as "useless" or feels sympathy for the accused. In
official parlance, he is sanukanpitawa salakā bälimen [giving
sympathetic consideration to the offender].

The relationship between the AGA and the GS is one of mutual
dependence. The grama sevakas are the eyes and ears of the AGA
in the community, and in turn the AGA provides a protective
shield for the GS. Still, this shield is not always needed,
since many complaints against grama sevakas are so insubstantial
that the petitioner does not even show up for the scheduled
hearing. Other petitioners claim that the petition was the work
of another person entirely, a prank to discredit him with the
GS.

The various responses to petitions should be viewed in the
context of the sociocultural environment. A GS is usually an
outsider in his division, which typically comprises a village
which was divided into factions long before his arrival. This
minor official arrives, an outsider endowed with influence over
every sort of transaction with the administration. The
recommendation of the GS counts; it is a required formality even

with people who possess the power to influence a higher
official. In remote and isolated areas the GS has police
functions as well, which further increase his power. Finally,
since the GS is technically supposed to keep an eye on all
activity in his division, his support can provide a protective
shield for criminal activities.

From the moment of his arrival, the GS is drawn into the web
of local intrigue. Having no official living quarters, he must
board in someone's house, and as soon as he accepts residence,
he is the ally of one faction and the opponent of the rival
group. In addition, the longer his stay in a particular
division, the more personally involved he becomes in its
affairs, which inevitably influences his work. His meager
salary, on the average about Rs. 350/., is barely sufficient
even for an official without a family to support; this makes
village intrigues even more appealing, since they can prove a
source of income to the GS willing to turn a blind eye to
illicit liquor dealing and gambling. Such involvement helps to
identify the GS with a particular group in his division, and
further alienates him from the others.

Finally, regardless of his actions, the GS as an outsider is
the target of hostility. His enemies can always make it sound
as if he has contravened one rule or another, and thus petitions
are written against him. For example, a high-caste petitioner
who says, "The GS threatened to have me murdered by a durawē" is
aware that this is an insult which has greater significance than
the threat to kill itself, for a durawē is a person of lower
caste. This reveals the existence of caste conflicts as well as
the ill-feeling against the GS. Faced with ubiquitous
intergroup conflict, the official also becomes a target for
aggression among less powerful groups. Those lacking an "in"
with politicians use the petition as their main outlet for
hostility, and the petitions reflect their concern for the
prestige they have lost in village facional struggles.

An average of two months elapses before an inquiry is held into a petition, and during this time the GS and his allies may use physical force to silence the petitioner. They may also threaten him by using their influence with politicians. There is a third factor that may keep a petitioner from showing up at the inquiry: merely writing the petition will have allowed him to vent his hostility toward the GS, but the fear of having to face him in subsequent interactions may deter the petitioner from following through. If he need not personally confront the accused, he can always deny having sent the petition.

Even when an inquiry does indeed take place, the petition is often dismissed for lack of substantiating evidence. In this case, the petitioner has one other possible source of satisfaction: he may take political action. Hence the common threat, petsamen bärinam dēsapālanayen [if not by petition then through politics]. Still, the petition is an important source of access to the administration for the client since it is available to all and, unlike political alliances, it has no price. The petition is also a way of buttressing self-respect; whether it succeeds or not, the fact of having written and sent it is important in itself.

For the GS, meanwhile, the petition serves as an outlet for complaints to his superiors about clients. He can vent his frustration over the inescapable political pressures brought to bear on decisions which he feels are his alone. The AGA, on the other hand, views the petition as the client's challenge to his authority. All petitions are addressed to the AGA, and are thus an attempt to make him give redress to the unknown client who will otherwise challenge his power by turning to the politician. Politician/official interactions are the subject of the following chapter.

130

FOOTNOTES

1. Alles (1976) makes the following statement about the
Burghers:

>   At the turn of the 20th century the public
>   service which I joined in 1912 was overrun by
>   the Burghers who while kowtowing to the
>   Britishers treated their dark-skinned,
>   unfortunate Sinhalese and Tamil colleagues
>   patronisingly, if not contemptuously. Their
>   forte was backbiting with the sole object of
>   currying favor with the white man to show him
>   that the Sinhalese were a disloyal race....
>   The Burghers of today are indeed to be pitied
>   for they are suffering for the sins of their
>   haughty forebears.

2. This type of exchange is referred to in the Philippines
and elsewhere in South and Southeast Asia as Bazaar-Canteen
behavior (Riggs 1958:6-59).

3. Simon and Silva, referring to Jamis's extortion of gifts
from clients, say "It is not a gift but a bribe." Chandra,
meanwhile, refers to Kamala's acceptance of the king coconuts by
saying, "Now the clients will think that all the ladies in this
office accept bribes, like her."

4. Cement is required for funerals for lining the inside of
the grave prior to burying the corpse. This is regarded as an
essential part of burial rites in the low country of Sri Lanka.

5. Marx (1972:281-315), discussing the rationality of
violence, says that it is only in modern society that violence
is considered immoral and irrational; many simpler societies do
not share this view. In discussing premeditated rational use of
violence against local officials in Maaloth, he considers
violence a desperate attempt to attract the official's attention
when no other means are available. The chair was the most
frequently employed weapon, and people often said, "All the
officials care for are their chairs." The case of the Black
Bull is underlined with a threat of violence and, in spite of
the symbolic significance of the seat among officials in Sri
Lanka, the possible weapon in this case was the kris knife
rather than the chair.

6. This refers to the Buddhist monk who is not merely
active and concerned about affairs in his community, but who
also extends his participation to enrich temple and/or kinsmen
by supporting candidates for political office and then making
use of his ties with the politician.

7. The _grama_ _sevaka_ report popularly known as the character certificate is an essential perquisite to obtain goods, loans, or jobs. This certifies that a client is a resident of a particular GS division, is a law-abiding citizen, and is in need of the services he is requesting.

8. This refers to the occasional meetings between the additional government agent and the _grama_ _sevaka_, when any new directives or instructions from the Ministry of Home Affairs are transmitted.

CHAPTER 6

Accessibility:

Bureaucrats and Politicians

A staff officer is an administrator with executive
authority. He holds officer's status, considerably higher than
the clerks and minor employees. The following discussion deals
with the DRO/AGA, the additional GA, and the GA, who form
ascending links in the chain of the administrative
hierarchy.[1] The district-level party organizer, the MP, and
the political authority in an administrative district fall into
the "politician" category. Here we will examine the
interruption of administrative routine by the MP and the party
organizer, while the role of the political authority will be
describer later.

The interaction between the politician and the administrator
(Kearney 1963, 1966; Warnapala 1974; Samaraweera 1975; Leitan
1979) differs from interactions between client and official, and
among officials, in that the latter involve an exchange of
services (Grindle 1977:26-30). Among officials, interaction is
the result of mutual interdependence. A client, however, is
dependent on the official; he must get what he wants by giving
what he can to the official. But the relationship is also
mutual; the official's very position, as well as the symbolic
gratification he receives from his position, depends on the
service he can provide to his clients. This is also true of the
official's relationship with the MP. The latter, in order to
achieve his ends (whether they be giving jobs to supporters or
obtaining scarce goods for them or for himself), must go through
the formalities of bureaucratic procedure. But here the
dependency is reversed. To the MP, the official is necessary,
but he is merely a tool, not an omnipotent source of power and
authority. To the official, the politician is also an unknown,

but one who can use his political office to challenge the
administrator's authority.

The DRO/AGA

The quality of interaction between the politician and an
administrator of higher rank is described succinctly by a former
GA: "At the level of the AGA, where the politician intervenes
to make a negotiation, it is an order; but at the level of the
GA it becomes a request." A distinction must also be made
between the political power of the party organizer and that of
the MP. Interference by the former is resented and considered
illegal, since his is not an elected office; attempts are often
made to block such interference. The MP, however, is grudgingly
conceded the right to interfere, though his interference is
often considered unethical. In the words of AGA Somapala,

>The Academy teaches us new management
>techniques. But how can I do anything when I
>don't even have a hole puncher in my office?
>The first thing you do in any office is
>maintain a file. How can you do this
>without a hole puncher? When the environment
>is pleasant, one feels like doing a good job.
>As a first step, I wanted to move this office
>to a better building. But still there is no
>response. If I can do it by myself, I will
>do it. In any office there should be one
>immediate superior to whom one is directly
>responsible, and one has a definite sphere of
>work to do. But here it is not like this. I
>have to be responsible to the GA, the MP, so
>many people. Really, I should be responsible
>only to the GA, but then the MP also tells me
>to do this and that. Even this is excusable;

he is the elected representative of the
people. But now the party organizer also
comes to dictate to me. Now look at this
request for a liquor license. Wilson [the
government party organizer] wants this for his
relative. This tavern will be within a half-
mile of a school, a temple and a mosque. The
whole idea is to help his own people. I am
going to stick to the rules, inquire from the
community leaders in the area, and if they are
against it, I will refuse to recommend the
application. If he wants to transfer me, then
let him do so. I like to be transferred.

The AGA, alternating between the boredom of routine work in
which he feels like a "useless rubber stamp," and the
frustration of succumbing to the extra-legal pressures of the
parliamentary politician, is disgruntled and alienated from his
official role.[2] He is well down in the administrative
hierarchy, and incurring the wrath of the politician means
risking his job. He has no choice but to give in to the demands
of the politician. At the AGA's level, such political pressures
come in two forms. First, the MP's letter may force his hand at
nearly every turn. According to the normative rules of the
bureaucracy, it is up to the official to determine each client's
eligibility for a particular good or service. But, in fact, the
official is forced to give priority to those applicants who come
with a letter from the MP. While some of these clients may
warrant this particular service, it is not often the case; for
example, land which is earmarked for the landless often ends up
the property of those who already own land. Second, clients who
bring the letter for apparently trivial matters, such as the
transfer of a ration book, arouse the ire of the official. He
considers it an affront to his dignity since it tells the
client, in effect, that this official can be pushed around even
in trifling matters, and is thus a person of no consequence.

If the welfare aspect of the AGA's administrative duties is usurped by the MP's letter, the development aspect is effectively controlled by the MP's list. Though welfare tasks were originally the duty of the AGA's office, and still continue to predominate, in recent years economic development has become increasingly important. With the decentralization of the administrative machinery, additional decision-making powers have been diverted from the central government and vested in the regional administration of the kachcheri. A corollary to the decentralized administration is a decentralized national budget. The financial outlay for each administrative division is done on a regional basis, and the local politicians and administrators are given charge of its implementation. Special emphasis is placed on agricultural development and cottage industries, large sums of money being devoted to the construction, repair and restoration of irrigation works, the purchase and distribution of agricultural implements and seeds, the provision of raw materials, and the provision of assistance to industries in setting up manufacturing, transportation and marketing of their products. In addition to using the existing rural development societies, these newly delegated development tasks lead to the creation of new structures at the administrative divisional level. These include the cultivation committees, the agricultural productivity committees, and the janatā [people's] committees.

Cultivation committees were originally made up of farmers elected from among their peers. The committees were supposed to coordinate and streamline rice production and to provide an institutional body wherein the farming interests could express their opinions. Over the years, however, the membership has been broadened to include others -- traders, for example -- on the MPs' recommendation. The agricultural productivity committees (five in this case), meanwhile, serve as coordinators for the different cultivation committees in a given region. It is the task of these committees to see that irrigation

facilities are provided, canals repaired, and seeds and
implements provided on time. Each agricultural productivity
committee is made up of a chairman and five other members.
Although it was envisaged that the membership of the committees
should also comprise those sympathetic to agricultural
interests, this has not always been the case.

In the selection of both cultivation and productivity
committees, the administrators are asked to submit a list of
suitable nominees. The MP asks the GA to submit a list, and the
GA assigns this task to the AGA. He, in turn, relies on the
recommendations of the GS. However, the determining factor is
the MP's recommendations, drawn from a list the MP himself makes
out while the official process is underway. Those named in the
MP's list approach him while he, meanwhile, checks the
applicants' political credentials rather than their suitability
for the posts. The MP chooses the finalists from the
administrators' list, having deleted some names and added
others, who may or may not qualify according to the proper
criteria.

Large sums of money pass through the hands of these
committees. They are given contracts for building works, and
are supplied with costly tools and implements and scarce
commodities such as cement. Accounts have to be maintained, and
the committee members are technically answerable to the AGA.
However, they are the MP's men, and monies are not always
properly accounted for. Projects in which many thousands of
rupees have been invested fall apart in six months; the cement
allocated for these projects has meanwhile "disappeared," while
the seeds, fertilizer and implements for which money was
allotted never reach the farmers. In the words of the AGA,

> These APC members are rogues. They are all
> an MP's henchmen. Now in this APC committee
> there is a baker and a bus driver. What kind
> of interest do you expect them to have in
> cultivation? For them it is another way of

making a quick buck. The other day I had to
inspect an anicut which was said to have been
repaired by the APC, prior to sanctioning the
payments. On closer inspection I discovered
that they [i.e., the APC] had merely placed
some sandbags against the wall of the anicut
instead of cementing it.

The rural development societies predate the APCs.
Originally they were meant to include village leaders who could
mobilize the community for self-help development projects.
Today, however, traditional village leadership having eroded,
the societies have become arenas for power politics. Nominally,
the AGA forms an RDS by calling for applications from qualified
persons. Those selected should be socially accepted village
leaders with the enterprise and initiative required to harness
village resources -- human and material alike -- for
development. In fact, however, applicants must "qualify" by
being on the MP's list. In return for being appointed to the
societies, the members must see to it that the societies'
meetings provide the MP and his party with a political platform,
especially on the eve of a general election. The meetings of
these societies actually increase in frequency around election
time.

A final example concerns the appointments to the janata
committees. These "peoples'" committees were established to
supervise and check the performance of government institutions.
Normally, it is the AGA's task to select applicants for
membership from among those responsible citizens whose personal
integrity is beyond question. However, the MP's list overrules
the AGA's in this case as in other appointments. In fact, on
one occasion when the AGA asked the GS for his recommendations,
he met with this cynical response: "It is a waste of time and
effort. Whatever we say, it is the MP who is the final
arbitrator." The AGA replied that it was nevertheless a
requirement, and that it had to be submitted though it was not
likely to be the deciding factor.

Selection of janatā committee members via the MP's list does not necessarily yield a group of men famous for their integrity and honesty. The committees are an object of ridicule in the community, where the general feeling is that "the biggest crooks are in the janatā committees." According to a grama sevaka, "If you are looking for a janatā committee member, you can sure find him inside a co-op," implying that said member would not be there in a supervisory capacity, but to acquire for himself the otherwise hard-to-find items sold by the co-op. In exchange for this, the co-op members expect him to turn a blind eye to their racketeering and black marketing.

Confronted with the MP's controlling influence on resource allocation and committee appointments, the AGAs are often frustrated men, thwarted in their attempts to exercise what they view as their legitimate statutory functions. Attempts to counteract the MP are to no avail. AGAs are petty officials, usually lacking their own political clout; unable to depend on protective support from their superiors, they must depend on their own salaries. This is revealed in an AGA's advice to grama sevakas; he warned them to be particularly careful of their actions, especially with regard to the MP, because "unlike in other days, the GA will not protect us today." AGAs frequently criticize the GA and the kachcheri, unhappy with the vague orders with which they are forced to comply and hostile over the fact that they must bear much of the burden technically assigned to the GA.

To be ordered about by the MP is excusable, but this is not the case with the party organizer. The latter's link with the party in power is his sole claim to authority. AGA Douglas had an encounter with the party organizer for the Ganvälla electorate, over the kachcheri office building. From the time of his predecessor, Somapala, constant attempts to shift the AGA's office to a better building, one with adequate space and proper ventilation, had been underway. Soon after Douglas assumed his duties, the GA and the minister of public administration finally

granted approval for a move and allocated funds for this
purpose. A modern building in the heart of the town was
earmarked for the offices, the AGA and the building's owner came
to an agreement, and a date was fixed for the move. Two weeks
prior to that date, the party organizer came to AGA Douglas's
office and said to him,

> You and I, we are relations [i.e., fellow
> caste members, as for that matter was the
> owner of the building in question]. We can
> fight over this all we want and you might even
> scold me. But there is an election around the
> corner, and one cannot predict its outcome. I
> may win or lose, but I cannot let you move
> into that building under any circumstances. If
> you do that, my opponents will say that I
> favored a kinsman and obtained the government
> lease for his building. You may do what you
> will after the election, but now I have told
> the GA to stop the move.

The fact remains that even though the owner of the building was
a caste brother of both the party organizer and the AGA, his
political allegiance was openly in the opposite camp. The fact
that the party organizer prevented the move served both to
punish the AGA for his political opposition, and to demonstrate
the party organizer's power over the GA, the AGA, and the owner
of the building.

Another motive for putting an end to the move was suggested
by the officials in the AGA's office. Next to the current
location of the office there is a tea stand owned and run by the
party organizer's chauffeur. The mainstay of its income is the
patronage of the officials and their clients. The officials
often complain about the exorbitant price of a cup of a tea, but
the convenience of the kiosk outweighs their objections. The
chauffeur was believed to have pressured the party organizer to
keep the AGA's office in its present location. The AGA himself,

though annoyed enough to refer to the party organizer as "that bloody fool" behind his back, was obviously powerless. He did his best to save face by saying, "This is only temporary. We have merely postponed the move for the time being."

The Additional Government Agent

At this level, the attitude towards political interference varies from resigned acceptance to open defiance. Thus, Additional GA Wimalasiri summed up his feelings in this way:

> Now, an officer is very careful in making a decision. He always consults the MP in advance in order to avoid the embarrassment of being reprimanded. Because of this, the officer might make a decision that goes against his own conscience. He can be transferred; he has no personal interest in the issue and he always has to make a decision which satisfies the government. At the same time, if the official antagonizes the MP, the latter can report him to the minister and get him transferred, and he will lose his salary increments and scholarship benefits. So, why bother? The other day, the MP for Kadugama wanted us to take over land belonging to his political opponents, ostensibly under the Land Reform Act. Under this act, one can only take over unused, uncultivated land but this was a very productive coconut property. We pointed this out to the MP, but it was to no avail. And look at this case: Mr. Newton Goonesekere is a good friend of the MP. They live in adjoining properties. Mr. G. is a realtor and also a car salesman. He recently obtained a car for the MP.

This statement is a prelude to the following.

Case Thirty. A client asks the Additional GA whether it is possible to stop the acquisition of a piece of land under the Land Development Ordinance once Section 2 has been gazetted [referring to a legal step in the process of acquisition]. The client says, 'This is that land in which the MP was keenly interested.' The Additional GA says that he remembers: 'He came here personally and endorsed it, and said that the takeover was an urgent matter.' The client says that he has spoken to the MP, and '[I] told him that I would like to buy this land and asked whether it was possible to stop the takeover, and he agreed to do so. I came to you to see whether this is really possible without unduly embarrassing the MP, especially these days.' Since it is election time, the Additional GA agrees that it would be difficult and embarrassing to take action at this time: 'He could be charged with bribery for planning the takeover and then going back on his plans.'

The Additional GA, alluding to the Land Reform Ordinance, tells the client, 'Now, you have to refer to Section 35. Only the minister of lands can stop it, and for that there must be sufficient pressure from the community itself not to warrant the acquisition. How can the MP, who strongly advocated it, now go back to the minister and tell him not to do it? One thing he might be able to do is to get a letter from local pressure groups, like party youth leagues and rural development societies, saying that they don't favor the takeover of this land because it is unsuitable for some reason, and then the minister can drop the acquisition. Another thing is possible. The land commission's department is for some reason slow on acting on these things. You can rest assured that, unless the MP himself goes again and pushes the case, the land might not be acquired, and then it is a matter for the next government.' The realtor nods his head and says, 'That won't help, because I have a good buyer for the land right now.' The Additional GA

replies, 'What you can do is to get the MP to submit a letter of
the kind I mentioned. MP X recently did this. He was pressing
for the takeover of a particular piece of land and then he got a
house as a gift from the landowner. Then he got a similar type
of letter, dropped the matter, and then advocated the takeover
of another piece of land instead.

This case shows an official's passive acceptance of the MP's
interference in the process of land acquisition; the acceptance
is so wide-ranging that the official acts as an advisor on how
to extricate the MP from a potentially embarrassing situation.
Ostensibly, the land reform commission was to acquire excess
land -- an individual being allowed to own 50 acres -- and
uncultivated land, neither of which applied in the above case.
Yet the official is unable to override the authority of the MP,
whose original purpose in seeking this acquisition was personal
revenge on a political opponent. Meanwhile, the situation was
complicated by the fact that an ally of the MP was intent on
acquiring the land in question. The Additional GA is thus
placed in the position of advising this client on how to
extricate his friend, the MP, from this difficulty.

Together with the letter and the list, the acquisition of
land under the Land Development Ordinance and Land Reform Act is
a source of power for the MP. He can force an official to take
over lands belonging to his political opponents, and he can also
force the official to distribute such land according to the
interests of the MP and among his allies (pandam kārayāo,
literally, torch bearers), rather than according to the
statutory criteria of need.

The actions of the Additional GA who preceded Wimalsiri
offer a contrast. One of seven MPs in the administrative
district and a member of the landed aristocracy, he decided to
donate an estate to the nation. His ostensibly charitable act
was given due publicity in the press, and it was announced that
the land was to be divided among the local landless poor. A

formal ceremony in which the land was to be given over to the
government was scheduled. A week before the ceremony, however,
the MP came to the AGA's office; finding the AGA away, he left a
message that he would be coming to see the AGA early the next
day. The MP came the next morning, and left quickly. Looking
pensive, the AGA explained,

> That was Podisingho. He has donated to the
> government a property of his in Gandarahena.
> He wants a permit to cut 16 jak trees on the
> property before it is handed over. Unlike
> other trees, a jak tree has great food value,
> and therefore we don't give permits to cut
> them unless a tree is dying or in danger of
> collapsing and harming property or people. A
> permit to cut a single tree is given only
> after careful inquiry. So I told him that I
> did not have the authority to give him the
> permit, and told him to speak to the
> Additional GA.

A few days later, I asked the Additional GA what had
happened in his meeting with MP Podisingho. Since people are
fearful of discussing political interference in administrative
routine, he was surprised at first that I was aware of the
case. He then told me,

> I explained the position to him. I told him
> that I consulted the GS, who informed me that
> the people of the area are opposed to his
> cutting the 16 jak trees and that I could not
> authorize the request. At this, the MP became
> angry and said, 'I am a government man. I
> will go to the minister and get this done, and
> I shall also see that you are sent on a
> punishment transfer.' I stood my ground and
> told him to do as he wished. Often they try
> to scare us with idle threats. Without some

> legitimate grounds, not every MP can carry out
> such a threat. Besides, if an officer himself
> knows and has the confidence of a senior
> politician -- as I do with the Minister of
> Highways and Power -- he can go ahead and
> stand by a decision without fear. I have
> personally known the minister since the days
> when I worked in the northwestern province.
> He is honest, an individual with integrity.
> If it came down to it, I could count on his
> personal knowledge of me and my work.

In the final analysis, the MP either could not or did not carry
out his threat of having the official transferred, but he did
get an order from the minister of lands enabling him to cut and
transport the 16 jak trees.

It was the AGA who took the consequences. Because of his
more immediate contact with the community, he incurred the wrath
of the public. Soon after the MP had the trees cut down, the
remaining trees were also chopped down and the logs from them
were discovered, by the GS, in the private yard of the chairman
of the local village council. When questioned by the GS, the
latter produced a permit authorizing his actions. The permit,
however, was signed by the chairman himself, acting in his
official capacity. This created an uproar among the members of
the local community, who submitted a petition to the
AGA/Additional GA and sent copies to the MP for the area -- not
the MP who donated the land in question -- and to the Minister
of Lands. The petition read as follows:

> A representative of the village council has
> cut down 16 jak trees from this land. This is
> public property which he has thus taken.
> People have protested against it but the
> officials have not taken any action against
> the culprit. There is a rumor spreading in
> this area that this is because two cartloads

of firewood were brought to your bungalow and
that is why you have not taken any action. We
thought you were an honest man. With all this
interest in the 'food drive' by the government,
you should try to conserve food trees like the
jak. To let a selfish individual destroy
government property like this is a grave
offense. You allowed this offender to get
away, yet when we come to you to get a permit
to cut a single jak tree which is endangering
our home or property, you make us face such
inconvenience. A copy of this letter is sent
to the GA, the MP, and the Minister of Lands.

The outcome was an order from the Government Agent that the jak
logs be confiscated from the village council chairman and the
culprit sued. But there was no sign that such action was ever
taken.

Thus, an act of dubious ethics on the part of the MP,
against which officials were powerless, was made the
responsibility of the AGA. In interaction between an official
and a member of parliament, the former is the lower unless he
himself has his own source of parliamentary political power to
back him up, as the Additional GA had in the earlier case. AGA
Douglas's often repeated words perhaps express the position of
the AGA best: "api tamayi häma ekatama hira vennē; apē bellē
tamayi tonduva vätennē [We get caught for everything; it is on
our own necks that the hook falls]."

The Government Agent
and the District Political Authority

The government agent is the official in charge of an
administrative district. His political counterpart in the
district is the district political authority (DPA). According
to a GA Workshop Report (1975:3),

It is well known that often government MPs
were consulted before even the GAs themselves
were appointed to their districts. The
independent, aloof, totally impartial GA had
become a myth several years ago. Obviously,
the extent of power and influence exercised by
the GA in comparison with that exercised by
the local politician, before and after the DPA
was set up, is very considerable. Yet one may
feel that the line should have been more
appropriately drawn, not at October 1973 [when
the Political Authority system was created],
but in 1970 or even 1956...even before the
creation of the District Political Authority,
the local politician did have effective
influence over the GA. The local politician
played an important role at the District
Coordinating Committee and District
Agricultural Committee meetings where
important decisions were taken...consequently,
one GA has said, 'The peoples' representatives,
namely the member of the National State
Assembly, became more the agent of the
government than the GA himself.' Hence what
we call the DPA today is only the result of
institutionalization of a hitherto different
political authority.

The DPAs were considered essential in order to make the
administration more responsive to the demands of the electorate,
especially in performing tasks associated with economic
development. It was created almost over night, in October,
1973, not by law or ordinance, but by a fiat of the Prime
Minister. A government MP was appointed the district political
authority for each of the 22 administrative districts, and the
choices were based on the PM's personal trust and confidence in

these men. Through subsequent circulars, the DPAs' authority
was made specific only in the case of the Food Production Drive,
the Decentralized Budget, and Land Reform. Again, the Workshop
Report states that

> It is surprising that when this new
> institution was originally set up in October
> 1973, no GA was given any set of instructions
> as to how this role and function was changed
> by the establishment of the DPA...the new
> system was set up more or less over the phone,
> with barely any reference to the Ministry of
> Home Affairs whose representative is the GA
> ....Circulars and instructions followed
> several weeks afterwards, but even these left
> vital questions unanswered. As a result,
> there were many instances of friction between
> the DPA and the GA as both parties had
> different interpretations of their respective
> roles. This resulted in the DPA interfering
> with the 'statutory'[3] and administrative
> actions of the GA. The general consensus is
> that the DPA has no statutory function, but
> unfortunately few DPAs appreciate this
> position. The rest act on the presumption
> that they have statutory authority to issue
> orders to Government Agents and other
> officials over their statutory duties. As can
> be imagined, this led to a situation, for
> example, where the DPA had issued 'orders' as
> regards authorized dealers [for food and other
> goods], or the transport of fish, and if these
> are not implemented, the GAs can be accused of
> non-cooperation and sabotage, an unenviable
> situation for the GA (Ibid.).

'Impeding factors' in the relationship between the GA and the DPA include such situations as the following.

> ...the frequency in the change of priorities
> as a result of the DPA diverting funds from
> originally specified purposes. As a result,
> differences of opinion arise between the DPA
> and the GA as accounting officer. Here again,
> the constant shift of priorities is an
> indication of the responsiveness of the DPA to
> varying political situations. He is less
> concerned with optimum resource allocation and
> use through the budgetary program
> implementation process than in satisfying
> immediate political needs....Another impeding
> factor cited is that the discipline and work
> preference of officials has been adversely
> affected because of their loyalties being
> divided between the DPA and the GA. This is
> ...a result of the tendency of certain DPAs to
> build up coteries of officials having either
> political or personal loyalty to them...this
> ...has frequently impeded corrective action
> being taken by the GA against government
> departments and other institutions such as
> co-ops. Where irregularities have been
> detected in these bodies, some DPAs have been
> found fighting hard to protect their
> loyalists, from the consequences of the
> actions. 'My men can do no wrong' seems to be
> the motto, and the GA is expected to detect no
> wrong where 'my men' are concerned (Ibid.).

The tension generated in such a situation can well be imagined. The GA Workshop Report further states:

> The general public prefers to seek assistance
> from the DPA even in matters over which

authority statutorily rests with the GA. This
is partly because politicians keep an open house
for all conceivable types of public complaints
and these are readily entertained by them.
In the view of the public, the DPA appears to
be an all-powerful person controlling the
district administration....On the whole, a
majority of the GAs have expressed that they
feel that their official prestige has been
reduced by the DPA.

These quotes are selected from the report submitted by the
GA Workshop and based on an opinion survey among the GAs of the
22 administrative districts. They vividly describe the role of
the politician vis-à-vis the GA prior to the DPA, and since
its institution. They reveal a clear erosion of the GA's
power. This is especially significant considering the powerful
and authoritative origin of the GA's position as the sole
representative of the British Crown, and later of the national
government, in the provinces.[4] Together with the loss of
official prestige is an interference with what the GA considers
his statutory functions, especially his disciplinary control
over his subordinates. All this amounts to a loss of the
prestige originally possessed by the GA. In the words of a
former GA,

The GA was the chief organizer in the
district. The relationship between him and
the politician was quite clear. The MP was
usually junior [in age] to the GA and regarded
himself as such in the latter's presence. He
addressed the GA as 'Sir.' The GA always
presided at functions and meetings, and the MP
welcomed him. The relationship was quite
clear as to who was the boss -- even if the MP
was a member of the cabinet. Now the position
of the MP and especially the DPA has been

> enhanced, from merely being a chap who raised
> his hand and decided legislation to a source
> of power.

This accurately describes the situation in the Ganvälla administrative district. Conforming to the often-expressed sentiment among the officials that the amount of actual political power wielded by the DPA depended on his personality, this politician, unlike many of his counterparts, used his office as a source of power to such an extent that officials were frightened of even mentioning his name in conversation. One of the DPA's first acts was to call himself not desapālana adikāriya [used by DPAs of other areas, and the Sinhala equivalent of the term 'DPA'], but disāpalana adikāriya [district ruling authority]. This change echoes the most common Sinhalese equivalent of the term disāpati [government agent], which strictly translates as "ruler of the district." The kachcheri is commonly referred to as disāpati kāriyālaya [office of the district ruler]. Paradoxically, this DPA's office was located in the same spot as the kachcheri, just across from the GA's office, and was called disāpalana adkāriya kāryālaya [office of the district ruling authority]. A former GA remarked that this change of designation symbolized the wresting of power and prestige from the GA by the DPA:

> By using the term disāpālana instead of
> desapālana, the DPA is in fact putting the GA
> in a subordinate position. The desapālana
> adhikāriya made little sense to the ordinary
> people, while the disāpalana adhikāriya did.
> The DPA has no fixed body of rules to operate
> with, so an attempt is made to give him a
> legal personality. There is no reference to
> the DPA in legislation, but there is plenty of
> reference to the GA.

The change also has tremendous symbolic significance in the minds of the citizens. By adopting the title disāpalana adhikāriya, being located next to the GA's office, and calling

his office that of the "district ruling authority," the DPA has
effectively eclipsed the GA. He has usurped that set of values
and expectations, backed by more than a century of tradition and
experience, associated with the government agent. In the words
of the GA Workshop Report, "the overwhelming impression created
is, however, that the people have rightly or wrongly come to
believe that the DPA is the chief government decision maker in
the district (Ibid., p. 28)." Prior the beginning of my
research, the DPA of the district had secured the transfer of
the previous GA as an act of vengeance. In fact, at formal
meetings the DPA would often mention this, as a threat to other
recalcitrant officials: "disāpālana adikāriya gānakata gannē
nä, hitan innava disāpālana adikāriya sellam baduvak kiyā,
mārurkarala dānava [Never listen to the DPA, think that the
district authority is a mere plaything, and you will get
transferred]."

During the time of my research, the GA in the Ganvalla
district was an administrator who had held a responsible
position in a very important ministry in the central
government. He had held the post for eight months at the time
of my arrival. His attempt to revive the lost authority of the
GA was evident in a circular he sent to his subordinates:

Allocation of Duties

One year has elapsed since my circular. The
time is opportune to reiterate some of the
matters referred to therein.

From 1/10/76 I will personally handle the
following: (1) food control; (2) land reform;
(3) food production.

My other subjects I shall handle through
the Additional GA and AGA (Headquarters), who
in turn will handle them through the staff
officer in charge of the branches in the
following manner: I shall as occasion demands
call for papers directly from the Staff

Officer in charge of the branches and the SO
shall feel free to see me directly on any
matter. When an existing principle is raised
and a new precedent created, the Additional GA
or the AGA must consult me. [Land]
acquisition proceedings must commence only
after my approval is obtained.

In regard to correspondence from the
general public, I expect a final reply within
five days of receipt of the letter in the
kachcheri. If this is not feasible because
more information has to be obtained to provide
an answer, an interim reply must be sent
within three days. I do not think that this
idea is impractical....Letters should be
worded in courteous terms and if relief cannot
be granted, full and convincing reasons must
be given....I have noticed cases where letters
to MPs have been perhaps unwittingly signed by
the Staff Officer. My rule was that all
letters to MPs should be put up for my
signature, and this includes also information
copies of letters.

The Government Agent/Cooperative Authority
vs. the District Political Authority

At our very first meeting, the GA, obviously ill at ease and
under pressure from the DPA, made the following comment:

I don't know whether you are aware -- Now we
have two newly created positions, the DPA and
the CA, the Cooperative Authority. The former
is the MP of Ganvälla, and the latter is the
GA. The PM realizes that the co-ops are
critical for the people's existence and that

there was a lot of corruption and exploitation
there, so the CA was formed under emergency
regulations as a structural counterpart to the
DPA. I am the secretary and accounting
officer of the DPA, and Mr. G [the
Headquarters AGA, who is the official in
charge of the administrative routine of the
DPA meetings] is my officer. He works under
me and takes orders from me, not from the PA.
On one occasion I told the DPA that as the
CA, I am not responsible to him: I am
responsible only to the Minister of
Cooperatives. He said, 'Why is this?
Everyone else consults me before making a
move.' He reported me to the Minister of
Public Administration. I meanwhile
reported what had happened to the Minister of
Cooperatives, and his secretary wrote back to
say that I need not report to the DPA. When I
told this to the DPA, he said, 'I can't take
the secretary's word for it.' He said that
the minister himself should write directly to
me. Now, why should the minister write to me?
The whole problem is that the previous GA gave
in to the DPA too much, and this has set a
precedent.

To prove his point, the GA proceeded to show me the
Cooperative Authority Emergency Regulations as set forth in
Public Security Ordinance No. 199/ICA, dated January 20, 1976:

(1) These regulations may be cited as
Emergency Co-op Authority Regulations. (2)
These regulations shall have effect
notwithstanding anything in the Co-op
Societies Law No. 5, 1972. (3) For each area a
Co-op Authority who shall be a body corporate

consisting of not more than five members
will be appointed by the Minister [of co-ops],
one of whom will be the president of the
Authority [the GA]. (4) The Minister may give
the Authority general or special directions in
writing as to the regulation of procedures in
regard to the meetings of the Authority. The
Authority shall have the following power:
(a) To issue instructions to cooperatives,
financial management, recruitment,
appointment, promotion, transfer, termination
of services of such societies; (b) To direct
the Board of Directors of any such co-op to
furnish their returns, accounts or other
information with respect to the property or
business of such a society; (c) To take over
conduct and management of societies of any
activity or to make alternate arrangements for
the conduct and management of such activity;
(d) To remove any or all members of the Board
of Directors without reason therefore and
appoint a person in place of a member who has
been removed from office. When all the
members of the Board of Directors have been
removed, to make suitable arrangements for
the management of such a society; (e) To
redefine the area of operation of any such
society.

It is the duty of the Board of Directors
of any cooperative to which instructions or
directions are issued to comply with them.

Those removed from office will vacate
office from the date of such removal,
notwithstanding anything in any other law, any
act or thing done by the Authority in the

> essence of the powers vested in it under
> Regulation 5, and by the Board of Directors of
> any co-op society for the purpose of complying
> with or giving effect to any instruction or
> direction issued by the Authority, shall be
> valid and effective and shall not be called in
> question in any court or tribunal.

The statistics in Appendix 2 indicate the scope and
magnitude of the cooperative movement in terms of financial
resources and personnel. Originally a citizens' self-help
movement, during the First World War it was converted to a state
organization for the distribution of rationed supplies. It
remains so to this day. Co-ops have also become valuable power
resources in the hands of politicians in recent years. The
politician can dispense favors to his allies [and thus buy
himself support] by granting them jobs in co-ops, in positions
ranging from casual employee to member of the board of
directors. Where vacancies do not exist, the politician can
create new co-op stores, whether there is a need for them or
not.

For those who secured jobs at co-ops through an MP, co-ops
proved a further source of income beyond their wages. Scarce
goods (often imported and then distributed only through co-ops)
often did not reach the shelves, but were sold under the counter
or to private dealers, who then marked them up to double the
original price. Corruption and malpractice were the order of
the day. According to the Ceylon Observer of January 2, 1977,
in an article called "Co-op Men Stage Hold-Ups," "The Criminal
Detective Bureau has expressed grave concern over the alarming
rate of cooperative robberies, some of which have been 'inside
jobs' causing heavy losses." Public hostility arising out of
this situation was general, and directed against the national
government, which was formally responsible for the co-ops. As a
result, the CA was created by the Minister of Co-ops after a
personal order from the PM to "clean up the co-ops." The CA was

made up of the GA, who served as president, the Assistant
Commissioner of Cooperative Development, and four other persons.

The CA audited the accounts of all cooperative societies,
and dissolved all but two of the co-ops in the Ganvälla
district. Their chairmen and directors were dismissed and the
societies were "blacklisted"; all government financial aid was
withheld until they were able to pull themselves out of the
red. Meanwhile, employees who were caught pilfering or
engaging in other forms of corruption were dismissed or
disciplined (e.g., ordered to make good the loss). Unproductive
co-ops were closed down. These actions, taken by the GA in his
capacity as president of the CA, aroused the wrath of the DPA.
According to the GA,

> Before the CA came into being, the board of
> directors and president of the co-op, as well
> as a lot of the employees, were appointed by
> the MP. They were his trusted lieutenants.
> Due to their corrupt practices, such
> appointees soon embezzled thousands of rupees
> from the co-ops. In quite a few cases I know
> of, they used this money to build themselves
> palatial residences, which were humorously
> referred to by the citizens as samūpakāra
> mandīra [co-op palaces]. As the CA...I
> dissolved the directorates of many of these
> co-ops. Those who were charged for the
> losses were given a deadline and told to make
> the payment in 10 installments over three
> months. I had to contend with the politician,
> in this case the DPA. He tried to show that
> his cohorts were paragons of virtue. He
> incited the employees who were sacked to
> organize a meeting against me, and he himself
> chaired it. They made representation to the
> Minister of Foods and Co-ops. The purpose was

to subordinate me to the DPA. I wrote to the
ministry for instructions:

'At the DPA meeting, the members of
parliament expressed strong disapproval over
the exercise of power of the Ganvälla DCA. It
was said that (1) the DPA was the sole and
ultimate authority in respect of all matters
in the district. The DCA should be subordinate
to the DPA. All decisions made by the DCA
should receive the concurrence and approval of
the DPA; (2) in matters of appointment to new
boards, recruitment of new staff, transfers,
etc., the MP should be consulted and his
approval obtained; (3) the Ganvälla DCA should
not be allowed to lay down general rules
regarding the conduct and management of co-op
societies which are not imposed on co-ops in
other districts.

As the powers of the CA are vested under
emergency regulations and cannot be questioned
in a court of law, it was not practical or
reasonable for the DCA to obtain the DPA's
approval....If there was one policy for the
entire country then there was no need to have
22 CAs....

I am willing to discuss any matter with
the MP or the DPA on subjects 1, 2, and 3, and
specific directions are requested from the
minister. Also, a strike threat has been made
by the employees of two multipurpose
cooperative societies in support of their
interdicted colleagues. Steps have been taken
to ensure an uninterrupted supply of food
rations to the public.'
The following reply to the above letter was

written by the secretary to the Minister of
Food and Cooperatives:

'...this minister has been entrusted
with the implementation of the proposals under
emergency regulations promulgated under the
direction of the PM. Any changes in the
instructions so long as they are within the
regulations should therefore emanate from this
ministry. Any changes will have to emanate
from the PM. This ministry has within the
framework of the regulations entrusted certain
functions to the DCA; since there have been no
variations in the instructions the DCAs
continue to be the competent authorities in
regard to those functions entrusted to them.

My minister has no desire to deprive
either the DPA or the MP of any privileges
they may be entitled to. However, it will be
repugnant to the emergency regulations and in
any case will go counter to the overall
objective that this ministry has, if the DCAs
are to be guided, directed and controlled by
any other authority than this ministry in
regard to cooperative matters. My minister
suggests that any questions the DPA may wish
to raise in regard to co-op matters should be
taken up at the political level with the
minister. When necessary, my minister will
issue suitable instructions to the DCAs in
regard to the matter.

However, in appointing people to boards,
one should not take in people who are
violently antagonistic to the government. In
the circumstances there can be occasions when
it may be prudent to seek the advice of the

PA, particularly to ascertain the political
acceptability of any given director.'

Despite this last word of caution to the GA, however, a
former GA told nme that "The CA gave new and tremendous
decision-making power to the GA. It was, in fact, a vote of
confidence in the bureaucracy by the community which said, 'we
trust you to think objectively.'"

The DPA, however, vented his frustration in a culturally
understandable and effective idiom: he used the monthly meetings
of the DPA as a public platform to openly ridicule the CA.
These meetings, chaired by the PA and with the seven MPs of the
district in attendance, were attended by the GA (who served as
secretary and accounting officer), the Additional GA, the
Headquarters AGA, the AGA, and all other government officials of
the staff grades. These included the assistant directors of
government departments and the Divisional AGAs. An average of
60 people attended each meeting, which constituted the monthly
face-to-face confrontation of the politician and the district
administrator. The purpose of the meeting was the politician's
review and evaluation of the progress being made in welfare and
development activities -- agricultural productivity, food
distribution, land allocation, and building construction --
within the administrative district. The meeting also served as
the time when recalcitrant or defiant officials received public
tongue-lashings.

At the time of this study, food distribution through the
co-ops took up much of the discussion. Typically, if the GA
(CA) was present, it was the Assistant Commissioner of
Cooperative Development (ACCD) who was questioned and who
supplied the answers. Though most of the officials chose to
keep silent and not contradict the DPA (rather than to risk
public ridicule), the ACCD always stood his ground in
confrontations with the DPA. The latter responded by attacking
the ACCD and his backer, the GA/CA. Still, the GA only received
requests; he did not take orders from the politician. In fact,

after the creation of the CA he was an equal of the PA, who,
forced to accept this fact, vented his anger on the ACCD, who
was clearly a subordinate. The GA/CA maintained his independent
stance, not coming openly to the ACCD's defense but watching as
he mounted his own public defense. This is revealed in the
following case.

Case Thirty-One. The DPA (who had been involved in some
non-profitable co-ops which had later been amalgamated) asks the
ACCD what the CA means by a 'viable' co-op. The official
replies that in order to be economically viable, a co-op needs
1,000 members. The DPA replies, 'I don't want to hear all this
talk. If it is 1,000 members you need, get them diverted from
those co-ops which have more.' The official interrupts, saying
that if a co-op has the required membership and the needed
buildings, he has no objection to keeping it going. The PA
says, 'Don't tell me those things. You have an adibalaya
[overriding authority] created under emergency power,' looking
at the GA, 'which does everything it wants. It won't listen to
even the people's representatives, dismisses and transfers poor
workers from the co-ops. Go tell him,' indicating the GA.

 The official again interrupts, saying that the suggestion --
that part of the membership of co-ops with more than 1,000
members be transferred to those with fewer members -- cannot
work: members are reluctant to be transferred to a co-op which
may be many miles from their homes.[5] The DPA replies, 'It is
because the people wanted them that we opened more outlets for
their convenience, and if you want to make it viable get your
authority to do what is necessary.' The official mentions the
need for more building space. The DPA replies, 'Don't ask us
for our buildings. Why, the CA has all the power, does he not?
Tell him to acquire anything and to make the necessary
arrangements.' The GA listens in silence.

Case Thirty-Two. On another occasion, the DPA asks the ACCD
what progress has been achieved in the reorganization of the
co-ops. The ACCD replies that a new wholesale co-op had been
opened. An MP who is present says, 'That is in my electorate.
How was it opened without my knowledge? This is incredible. We
are the people's representatives, and it is an insult to us that
we are not informed of what is going on in our electorate.
Close that co-op at once and sack the entire directorate!' The
DPA adds, 'Yes, this is to show the public that the people's MPs
(mahajana mantrī) have nothing to do with the co-ops, deprive us
of an opportunity to address a crowd and thereby deliberately
put us down.' The ACCD suggests that the co-op be closed down,
and then opened again in the presence of the MP. The DPA
insists that the co-op's manager should be fired. The ACCD then
says, 'If I do that I may as well get rid of the other members
of the board, and I don't know who else to appoint. In one more
month we will hand the societies back to the people.' (It is
worth noting that he uses the word mahajanaya -- people --
rather than mahajana mantrī -- MP.)

The politician is offended, and replies that this problem
does not concern him. He simply knows that the ACCD has made a
mistake, and wants to know what he intends to do about it. The
ACCD proposes to consult the CA (who is present but who does not
show any emotion or indeed, any support). The ACCD then looks
at the CA and says, 'I'm not the only one in this. There are
four others, also. I'll have to consult them.' The DPA insists
that the ACCD decide on his own, but the official stands his
ground. The politician, still offended, says, 'Now you accept
that what is done is värädda [wrong]. Tell the secretary to
note that down, that the ACCD accepts that what happened was
wrong (värädda piligena).' The ACCD stops him, saying 'I accept
that a lapse (adupādu) has taken place.'

At this, all the MPs are aghast. The ACCD repeats this,
saying that he will call for an explanation and discuss it with

his superiors. The DPA, furious, says, 'You mark my words. I will get rid of this whole set of officials from this district.'

A week after this incident, it is rumored that the GA plans to leave. The GA himself confirms this, saying that he had only come to the area for a short time and is returning to the X ministry, as soon as possible. It is rumored that he got the transfer through the minister of state, who is an old schoolmate. The DPA, meanwhile, boasts that he had the GA transferred because of the co-op fracas, but at the next DPA meeting expresses his sorrow at losing the services of so able a man as the GA. The politician even says that he tried to convince the GA not to leave, and he concludes his remarks by thanking the official for the great services he rendered to the community and the cooperation he extended to the representatives of the people.

By contrast, the GA's successor, a junior official newly promoted to the rank, came into office with the DPA's approval. The situation was further eased when the emergency regulations lapsed a few weeks later, thereby ending the special powers of the GA/CA. The co-ops reverted to the political control of the MPs and the DPA.[6] This new GA and his two predecessors provide a study in contrast. They all held a position which traditionally carried with it much power and prestige, but which was subsequently weakened by the power of the MPs and specifically, that of the DPA. The rationale for the creation of the DPA was that it would improve the coordination of development tasks at the district level. The GA was no longer able to control and supervise the activities of the government departments at the district level, because these department-level officers owed their allegiance to their departments heads in Colombo. This again goes back to the traditional rivalry between the liberal arts-educated civil servant -- the generalist of whom the GA is the best example -- and the specialist in technical services. The former was long used to being considered the cream of the administration, while

the latter were its dregs. As the state's development functions
multiplied and became diversified, the specialized services came
into their own, and the roles were reversed. Consequently, the
GA was unable to perform his supervisory and coordinating role
(cf. Leitan, 1979).

The predecessor and the successor to the GA/CA mentioned in
the above two cases were caught in this situation, crushed
between the parliamentary politician and the department
official. The GA/CA, on the other hand, was a senior
administrator chafing under the political pressures. He was
afforded an opportunity to test his power through the
specifically constituted CA. Having exercised this power, and
with the imminent lapse of the emergency regulations under which
his special powers were created, he faced an intensely vengeful
and hostile politician and the prospect of becoming again merely
a GA. Given this prospect, his transfer was a blessing.

The Government Agent as a Successful Strategist

Between the two extremes -- the GA who is a passive tool and
the openly independent official who infuriates the politician --
there is a middle way. In the words of a former GA,

> If the administrator understands the
> situation, things are not hopeless. He should
> realize where power lies and how he can
> contribute to it, even in the face of things.
> It requires the temperament to attune oneself
> to the realities of the situation. Rather
> than have ideas at variance, one must realize
> that this is the situation and now, what can I
> do about it? Once you understand that,
> without stooping you can build up the
> situation. You take into account the
> situation and inject your good ideas into the
> framework already provided by the MP. For

instance, MP X was a man full of good ideas.
He wanted to do a lot of good for his
electorate. All I had to do was show him I
was with him....After some time I had his
confidence. Having won [a politician] over,
you can even turn the tables on him. On the
way, you have to see to it that a few people
he is interested in are well treated. In the
old days, we had to be skilfull in horseback
riding; now we have to be skillful in
balancing all sides of the political field.
An official who is interested in his work and
understands the situation can have a
rewarding job. He has to understand the
political climate in which he works. The MP
knows his area but does not have all the time
in the world. He is in Colombo on certain
days, attending the assembly, sitting in
committees, even going abroad. All of this
means that he spends perhaps only the weekend
in his electorate. He is willing to listen to
the hard-working, intelligent administrator
rather than the stooge. There is a break in
communication between the bureaucracy and the
politician. It is up to the bureaucracy to
take up this challenge. You don't want his
favors. But you can use power for the public
good. The MP might want to give 500 acres on
a hilltop to some villagers, but if you can
convince him that this will lead him to such
and such a problem, then you -- the GA --
have won.

An official who works within the given constraints, with
confidence, initiative and enterprise, and without taking
personal offense at what is actually a readaptation of his role,

seems able to keep his self-esteem. He makes a successful
adaptation and is respected and consulted by the politicians,
rather than being at odds with them.

The Bureaucracy at Election Time

A crucial change in the mode of interaction between the
administrator, the client, and the politician occurs between the
date of the dissolution of parliament and the day on which the
general election is held. People who are relatively powerless
in the face of the bureaucracy suddenly achieve a sense of
power, real or imagined. They say to officials, "Wait until the
election, and I will get you transferred." I saw no instance
where this threat was successful, but at least it served to
given an otherwise powerless person a sense of power through the
vote.

During this same time, another set of people lose their
manipulatory powers. In the words of an administrator, "With
the dissolution of parliament, there are no MPs -- only ex-MPs
-- and so there are no MP's lists or letters." Without these
pressures, the administrator is left to work at his own
discretion, guided only by the administrative codes and the
general direction provided by the cabinet, the PM, and the
Minister of Public Administration. The administrator is also
free of other local pressures since, during this time of limbo,
all routine administrative tasks (handling permits and rice
ration books, and distributing goods and resources) are at a
standstill except in cases of emergency. The officials are on
election duty, compiling voting registers, and preparing ballot
boxes, polling booths, and so forth.

At this same time, politicians lose their powers.
Paradoxically, the politicians must depend on the administrators
to regain their power. It is the administrator who must conduct
the general election smoothly, efficiently, and impartially. In
addition, to the extent that he keeps the routine administration

running smoothly, the administrator lessens the chance of
hostility being aroused against the government. Finally, the
politician must hope that the administrator will not use his
position to influence voters against him; as the prime minister
said in an address to the GAs, cited in the Ceylon Daily News
(April 23, 1977), "[you must] not allow the administration to
slacken as a result of the forthcoming general election, but
continue the good work done in the past." The Minister of
Public Administration also paid tribute to the grama sevakas for
having fulfilled their duties in the past, and said that they
were again entrusted with the task of ensuring a "clean"
election.

In the words of an illustrious ex-administrator, speaking of
the role of the administrator during an election period,

> There is a crucial change of role from the
> date of the dissolution of parliament. This
> date tells the public servant that from there
> on, the country depends on him to ensure a
> smooth transfer of power. The normal routine
> is replaced by heightened activity during the
> pre-election months. The administrator has to
> cut corners and do things for the government
> in power; every act gets a political coloring.
> But he is also conscious of the future, of
> what will happen to him if he goes beyond the
> limit [i.e., if the opposition party comes
> into power]. Around election time the MP is
> also a candidate, and suddenly a strong public
> servant comes into his own. He can tell the
> ex-MP, "Let's put this off." The tendency is
> to treat all candidates alike, even opponents.
> The public servant becomes very conscious of
> his position; it is a very interesting role
> change. At the same time, the public changes
> its expectations. Those who are beyond the

pale of power wait for the one day when they
can exercise their power with the official;
they use this opportunity to make their
demands. The elections themselves are
conducted with a degree of detachment and
impartiality that is extraordinary. It tends
to be treated as another operation to be
performed. The decision is made by an outside
source [the voter], but you [the
administrator] see it through.

In this chapter, we have examined a different category of
the unknown -- persons with formal or informal political power
-- and the special nature of their relationship to the
administrator. A politician such as the party organizer
successfully completes a transaction for himself or on behalf of
a follower by manipulating the official. Since he does not hold
formal political office, his intervention is considered illegal
and therefore, openly resented. The intervention of the MP,
however, is accepted as his right but still resented.

The party organizer and the MP, like other unknowns, attempt
to gain access to the administrator in order to obtain goods and
services, but unlike other unknowns, they generally intervene on
behalf of their followers. This is resented by the official,
who views it as an attempt to tell him how to do his job. The
DPA institutionalized the existing practice of political
intervention, but the ensuing conflict between him and his
administrative counterpart, the GA, was largely due to the fact
that the former does not confine his intervention to matters of
development. Unlike the party organizer or the MP, the DPA does
not seek access to the administrator in order to obtain goods
and services; his goal is to obtain the symbolic, de facto power
and authority of the office. When the DPA succeeds, it means
embarrassment and loss of self-esteem for the official. This is
especially true when the politician challenges the official at
the monthly public meetings of the DPA. The creation of the

Cooperative Authority gave the GA an opportunity to respond to this challenge, if only temporarily.

The politician's entry into the administrative arena results in the storming of the bureaucratic persona. As in the case of a confrontation with a client using coercion through physical force, an official loses control over the process of accessiblity in his interactions with a politician who backs his demands with the coercive power of office. Though expediency does not always dictate it, an official can resort to police protection when threatened with physical force. When threatened with the politician's powers, however, the official must rely on fortuitous intervention by the political system, in the form of decisions by the Prime Minister or the process of preparation for the general elections.

FOOTNOTES

1. Between these two positions there are two others: the Headquarters AGA and the AGA of the entire administrative district. The former coordinates all divisional activities at the distict level, while the latter handles "land tasks." However, since they are not directly relevant to the purposes of the argument, they are excluded from this discussion.

2. Taub (1969) discusses the sources of structural constraint and stress on bureaucrats in the Indian Administrative Service.

3. Statutory duties concern licenses, permits for fire arms, and action taken under the Forest Ordinance, the Irrigation Ordinance, and the Crown Land Ordinance of Sri Lanka as it is applicable to the administrative district.

4. Leitan (1979:165-201) examines the changing role and functions of the GA from the colonial period on.

5. This was indeed the case, as it subsequently turned out. With the lapse of power of the CA at the end of Emergency Rule, the politician regained control of the co-ops. The AGA was faced with frequent complaints from clients demanding to know why their membership in a particular co-op (via the ration book) had been forcibly transferred to another co-op many miles from their homes. The AGA's reply is that he has no control over these matters, that the transfers were the MP's wish. The angry clients threaten to deal with the MP when he campaigns in their area prior to the next election.

6. The _Ceylon Daily News_ of October 23, 1976, reported that
    District Administrators -- government agents, assistant government agents, divisional revenue officers and _grama sevaka niladaris_ -- will not be allowed to hold office in co-operatives from January 1 next year except in special instances.

    Only those who are recommended by the MP for the area and the Minister of Food, Cooperatives, and Small Industries, will be allowed to continue to hold office. He explained that the reason for this decision was that these district officials holding such positions in co-ops often came into conflict with political authorities and MPs.

    Consequently, it hindered the more important task of implementing development programs, especially under the decentralized budget.

CHAPTER 7

Conclusion

Administrative behavior is a type of political behavior;
that is, it concerns the exercise of power. It is shaped by
cultural themes that are derived from concerns which far
transcend administrative settings. In this process, these themes
are transferred from the abstract world of mental forms to the
concrete realm of partisan struggle.[1] They provide the idiom
for implicit communication, and an understanding of them is
required to study access to the public official.

The kachcheri administrator in Sri Lanka is truly the
successor to the men who ruled[2] rather than the men who
administered. They are the inheritors of both a patrimonial and
a British colonial administrative legacy in which political
power was fused with administrative power and concentrated in
the hands of a single individual. Over the centuries, this
power was determined to varying degrees by the relative
influencee of four social institutions: patrimonial
administration, the caste system, Buddhism, and western
philosophical and liberal ideals epitomized in the colonial
civil service.

In the patrimonial system, administrative power was
distributed within an ascribed hierarchy, and positions were
held according to the caste ranking of the individuals, with an
expectation that decision making would be tempered by principles
derived from custom and from Buddhism.[3] There was
considerable individual discretion in the exercise of power,
often to the point of exercising absolute rule. But such power
was in principle exercised by the politician-administrator in
his capacity as protector of the community. Absolute political
and administrative power legitimized by caste ranking, tempered
by custom and Buddhism, and exercised for the protection of

society, were the essential characteristics of patrimonial administration in Sri Lanka.

In the colonial bureaucracy, power was the privilege of a class of men whose authority was derived from the rules and regulations of the colonial civil service. They were guided by a dual vision. One vision was that of Plato's State, "ruled by guardians who were especially chosen by their seniors in the service, trained in the use of their bodies and in the study of history, taught that they were a separate race from those they ruled, aloof . . . and governing by the light of what they knew to be beautiful and good" (Woodruff 1954:15). The other part came from utilitarianism: "a spirit which inquired skeptically whether an institution was defensible by human reason, whether it contributed to human happiness and whether it was consistent with a respect for the value of human beings as individuals. Sometimes critical of authority, they believed that the performance of duty was good in itself and this duty was the guardianship of subject peoples" (Ibid.).

From these patrimonial and colonial origins, there emerges the following picture of the civil service administrator in Sri Lanka. He exercised political and administrative power simultaneously. He worked within an authoritarian bureaucracy. He was constrained by custom and principles derived from Buddhism (the patrimonial part of the legacy) and by the utilitarian values of a rational bureaucracy (the colonial part of the legacy). It is the combination of these various institutional values that confers legitimacy on the modern official.

In Sri Lanka, as time passed and specifically, since the 1931 constitutional changes heralded by the Donoughmore Reforms,[4] the power of the politician-administrator was diminished in two ways. First, there emerged a new species, the native politician who ultimately secured political independence for the nation; second, many administrative tasks -- notably police and judicial functions -- were assumed by specially created departments. But while the powers of the administrator were being eroded, the legitimacy associated with his position was not. Herein lies the explanation for the conflict between the politician and the administrator. The former has political power, backed by force and coercive sanctions, but to a large extent he still lacks legitimacy (Bendix 1978:17). Given the sociocultural context, such legitimation can be acquired only at the expense of the administrator.

In interactions between administrator and client, there is a combination of formality and flexibility. Formality allows the administrator to close the door on the unknown client, but the system is flexible enough to allow exceptions. The patrimonial and colonial administrators (both native and foreign) were drawn from an exclusive ruling elite, and such exceptions were made for the fellow members of this elite. Nowadays, with the recruitment of officials from a broader range of society, notably the rural intelligentsia, the clientele claiming exceptional treatment in gaining access to an official has been expanded. This also means that a greater variety of rural cultural themes can be used to demand access. The present study was conducted in a region where 90 percent of the population is made up of low-country Sinhalese Buddhists; thus, the cultural themes expressed here are, naturally, rather specific to this population. A _kachcheri_ elsewhere in Sri Lanka -- for example, among a population of Tamils or Muslims, or even up-country Sinhalese -- might exhibit different patterns.[5] Moreover, the nature of the organization may also determine what kinds of cultural themes are easily accommodated. Thus, there are differences among the themes used in a provincial _kachcheri_, in its provincial counterpart in Colombo, in other government organizations, in state-owned corporations, and in private enterprises. Finally, not all themes are appropriate for

systematic use in the public arena. For example, caste
identification as well as membership in an official's immediate
family[6] was at no time used -- at least in public -- to claim
access to an official in the Ganvälla kachcheri.[7]

Many studies have been made of personalism in bureaucratic
behavior. Price (1975) shows how value associated with the
extended family in Ghana provides the primary motive for
personalization of administrative behavior. Presthus
(1962:1-23) discussed the impact of the value placed on
militarism, patriarchalism, age, and rank on a bureaucracy in
Turkey. Other studies indicate that Max Weber's concept of
'formalistic impersonality' and its accompanying rationale of
behavior is influenced either positively towards impersonalism
or negatively towards personalism by cultural themes in
particular social settings. Crozier (1964:220-24) explains that
bureaucracy in France reflects the French cultural practice of
conidering face-to-face dependent relationships as difficult to
bear and therefore to be avoided. As a result, authority is
converted as much as possible into impersonal rules. In
contrast, in Japan (Bellah 1957) the bureaucracy reflects the
values of the Samurai strata from which the upper echelons of
the civil service were drawn, values which include rationality
in bureaucratic work and the selfless fulfillment of duty
typical of a modern bureaucracy. In his study of a South Indian
bureaucracy, Heginbotham (1975:24-52) decribes a fourfold value
system derived from the Dharmas, British colonial bureaucracy,
Gandhian ideals, and principles of community development. He
contrasts notions of work as derived from Dharmic and Gandhian
ideals. The concept of kadamei, derived from Hindu philosophy,
is defined as work according to one's caste and family in return
for salary. The Gandhian notion of poruppu signifies work
according to one's conscience. Finally, Siffin (1966:130), in
his discussion of the Thai bureaucracy, states that official
behavior there is underlined by individual detachment between

men and the system, which in turn is derived from Buddhism:
"identity might derive from official status; the content of
one's primary rule in life may be bureaucratic; and mutual
well-being might depend directly and wholly upon one's
position. But one still remained an individual apart with a
limited sense of commitment or involvement."

Contrary to the evolutionary perspective (Riggs
1970:72-108), this study takes the position that one cannot
expect a steady development of rational bureuacracy, in which
the bureaucracy is able to change its environment. The
environment is a constraint. A formal organization is always --
though to varying degrees -- a creature of its cultural
context. The culture defines the nature and extent of
'formalistic impersonality,' which is the essence of a Weberian
bureaucracy. Despite the fact that welfare is one of its major
goals,[8] the central principle of the Sri Lanka Administrative
Service in defining the role of administrator is
impersonality.[9] But this aspect of the bureaucratic persona
is reserved only for clients deemed "unknown." There are
various degrees of accommodation made for the "known face" and
the "unknown helpless." In the final analysis, at the core of
administrative behavior lies the notion of a personal self in
opposition to the impersonal, faceless exercise of
responsibilties of office. These notions draw their resonance
from the culture rather than from the administrative structure,
and the "self" is based on an official's identification with one
or more social groups within the community.

In Sri Lanka, the actual patrimonial administration has
receded into the historical past. But the key institutional
principles that were part of it have remained as vibrant
cultural themes. In contrast, the colonial administrative
structure of the kachcheri has remained in existence. But the
majority of present-day administrators[10] subscribe not to the
visions of Plato and Bentham, but to certain other values
associated with the institutions of caste and Buddhism. Within

an administrative setting based on norms of rationality, the official distinguishes between the "known face," the "unknown helpless," and the "unknown." He does so because he has a notion of how the self should be reflected in the bureaucratic persona. The cultural themes at the root of this definition of self are caste and Buddhism. Caste and Theravada Buddhism may be incompatible at the level of dogma, but they are not so at the level of behavior. It may indeed be the case that in Theravada Buddhist Thailand, an administrator's individual identity is kept distinct from his position as an administrator, as Siffin claims. But in Buddhist Sri Lanka, administrative behavior is guided by other Buddhist ideals, such as pin [merit], karunā [compassion], and 'humanity before duty,' and these ideals are not detached, but rather are enmeshed in the position of administrator: the symbolic and political overtones of this attachment resemble a person's identification with his caste and its accompanying attitudes toward the self.

FOOTNOTES

1. This is a reformulation of Geertz (1972:320).

2. This phrase is borrowed from Philip Woodruff's work, The Men Who Ruled India. His description of the Indian Civil Service is easily transferable to a description of the colonial civil service in Ceylon.

3. According to Dewarja (1972:154-55), the king who was at the apex of the patrimonial political-administrative system was expected to govern according to the ten royal virtues: dana [charity], sila [piety], pariccaga [liberty], ajjava [candor], majjava [impartiality], tapa [self-control], akkadha [freedonm from anger], avihimsa [gentleness], khanti [patience], and avirodhata [non-violence].

4. For a discussion of the constitutional changes initiated by the Donoughmore reforms, see Warnapala (1974:;85-147).

5. I consider the distinction made between welfare and Weberian bureaucracy (Presthus 1962:v.6, 1-23) as a distinction between structure and goal rather than a distinction between two types of bureaucratic situations. The kachcheri in Sri Lanka is a Weberian type of bureaucratic structure with welfare as its original goal. This study has emphasized this goal at the expense of its other (recently acquired but no less significant) goal of development. The role of the administrator in development, the concept of development administration (Braibanti and Spengler 1963, Braibanti 1969, Riggs 1970), the choice between the goals of welfare and development, the machine-like behavior of the politician vis-à-vis development goals, are the subject of a different study.

6. While the kachcheri bureaucracy in Ceylon during colonial times may be characterized as a dual structure (Hoselitz 1963:168-96), what formally exists today is a single unified structure with formal rational principles as its cornerstone. The duality lies not in structure but in administrative behavior vis-à-vis access to the administrator, one for the "known face" and another for the "unknown."

7. There is a strong influence of the joint family among the Tamils in Sri Lanka, while among the Muslims there is a dominant matrilineal bias. Among the up-country Sinhalese, the Buddhist high clergy of the Asgiriya and Malwatta Chapters, as well as the Kandyan aristocracy, provide cultural themes absent elsewhere among the Sinhalese.

8. This includes the family of orientation as well as the family of procreation.

9. Barring ethnicity, caste provides the largest cultural categorization of persons, while the family provides the smallest. One explanation for the absence of open public claim on the basis of either is that, unlike the middle amorphous category of kinsmen, these categories are discreetly identifiable. Not asking for or granting special privileges on the basis of either reflects some awareness and ambivalence on the part of both client and official of the dual standards applied to the known and the unknown.

10. This refers to the post-colonial administrator who emerged from the rural intelligentsia. Exceptions are the few remaining administrators who had begun their careers in colonial times and continued to serve subsequently. In their case, it is appropriate to conclude that the admixture of values for the patrimonial and colonial legacies has continued to influence behavior.

APPENDIX 1

An Early Petition

Petition No.	014463/3335
Date of Reference	1881, Jan. 4
To Whom Addressed	To His Excellency the Government Agent
From Whom	Don Andiris Appu and 50 Others
Prayer	Praying for the inquiry regarding the overtaxing of certain lands.
To Whom Referred	To the Moodliyar of Ginnoruwatte (a native chief)
When Reported to the Government	1881, Feb. 1

SOURCE: Department of National Archives No. 27/274.

APPENDIX 2

Cooperatives in the Ganvälla Administrative District

Assets as of June 22, 1976

Members' deposits	Rs. 764539.81
Non-members' deposits	Rs. 1443656.60
Permanent deposits	Rs. 37156.56
Short-term loans given	Rs. 1110671.84
Pawn broking	Rs. 2448811.00

Staff Positions

Society	Authorized Positions	Unauthorized Positions
1	199	245
2	201	95
3	190	85
4	205	129
5	179	230
6	186	31
7	369	9
8	117	3

REFERENCES CITED

Abeyasinge, Tiriki
    1966   Portuguese Rule in Ceylon. Colombo: Lake House
            Publishers.

Administrative Report of the Government Agent
    1870   Colombo: The Government Press.

Alles, C.E.J.
    1976   The Burghers. In the Ceylon Daily News, September 10,
            Colombo: Lake House Publishers.

Anderson, Benedict R. O'G.
    1972   The Idea of Power in Javanese Culture. In Culture and
            Politics in Indonesia, pp. 1-69. C. Holt, ed.
            Ithaca: Cornell University Press.

Anonymous
    1963   The Public Servant: A Self-Portrait and a Self-
            Criticism. In The Public Service and the People.
            C.R. Hensman, ed. Colombo: Community Press.

Arasaratnam, S.
    1958   Dutch Power in Ceylon 1658-1687. Amsterdam:
            Djambatan Press.

Bailey, F.G.
    1963   Politics and Social Change in Orissa. Berkeley: The
            University of California Press.

    1970   Stratagems and Spoils. Oxford: Blackwell.

    1977   Morality and Expediency. Oxford: Blackwell.

Bailey, F.G., ed.
    1971   Gifts and Poison. Oxford: Blackwell.

    1973   Debate and Compromise. New Jersey: Rowman and
            Littlefield.

Bellah, Robert N.
    1957   Tokugawa Religion: The Values of Pre-Industrial
            Japan. Boston: Beacon Press.

Bendix, Reinhard
    1978   Kings or People. Berkeley: University of California
            Press.

Blau, Peter M.
    1963   The Dynamics of Bureaucracy. Chicago: The University
            of Chicago Press.

Blau, Peter M. and W. Richard Scott
  1962 Formal Organizations. San Francisco: Chandler.

Braibanti, R. and Joseph Spengler, eds.
  1963 Administration and Economic Development. Durham:
        Duke University Press.

Braibanti, R., ed.
  1969 Political and Administrative Development. Durham:
        Duke University Press.

Britan, Gerald M. and M. Chibrink
  1980 Bureaucracy and Innovation: An American Case. In
        Hierarchy and Society, pp. 61-72. G.M. Britan and
        R. Cohen, eds. Philadelphia: Institute for the Study
        of Human Issues.

Ceylon Daily News
  1976 District Officials Can't Hold Office in Co-Ops from
        January. (October 23) Colombo: Lake House.

  1977 The PM Addresses the GAs. (April 23) Colombo: Lake
        House.

Ceylon Observer
  1977 The Monopoly of a Few. (January 2).

  1977 The Co-Op Men Stage Hold-Ups! (January 2).

Cohen, Abner
  1974 Two Dimensional Man. Berkeley: The University   of
        California Press.

Cohen, A.P. and J.L. Comaroff
  1976 The Management of Meaning: On the Phenomenology of
        Political Transactions. In Transaction and Meaning:
        Directions in the Anthropology of Exchange and
        Symbolic Behavior, pp. 87-107. B. Kapferer, ed.
        Philadelphia: Institute for the Study of Human
        Issues.

Collins, Charles
  1951 Public Administration in Ceylon. London: Institute
        of International Affairs.

  1966 Ceylon: The Imperial Heritage. In Asian Bureaucratic
        Systems Emergent from the British Imperial Tradition,
        pp. 444-84. R. Braibanti, ed. Durham: Duke
        University Press.

Crozier, Michel
1963 The Bureaucratic Phenomenon. Chicago: The University of Chicago Press.

DeKrester, Bryan
1976 The MP's Letter. In the Ceylon Daily News, September 23. Colombo: Lake House.

de Silva, Chandra R.
1972 The Portuguese in Ceylon, 1617-1638. Colombo: H.W. Cave.

de Silva, Colin R.
1953 Ceylon Under the British Occupation, 1795-1833. Colombo: Apothecaries Press.

Dewaraja, Lorna S.
1972 A Study of the Political, Administrative, and Social Structure of the Kandyan Kingdom of Ceylon, 1707-1760. Colombo: Lake House.

Fallers, Lloyd A.
1965 Bantu Bureaucracy: A Century of Political Evolution Among the Basoga of Uganda. Chicago: The University of Chicago Press.

Fernando, P.T.M.
1970 The Ceylon Civil Service: A Study of Recruitment Policies, 1880-1920. In Modern Ceylon Studies: A Journal of the Social Sciences 1:64-83.

Geertz, Clifford
1973 The Interpretation of Cultures. New York: Basic Books.

Goffman, Erving
1959 The Presentation of Self in Everyday Life. New York: Doubleday, Anchor.

Goonewardene, K.W.
1958 The Foundation of Dutch Power in Ceylon, 1638-1658. Amsterdan: Netherlands Institute for International and Cultural Relations.

Grindle, Merilee
1977 Bureaucrats, Politicians, and Peasants in Mexico. Berkeley: The University of California Press.

Gunasekere, Leel
1973 Petsama. Colombo: Pradeepa Publishers.

Handelman, Don
  1976   Bureaucratic Transactions: The Development of
         Official-Client Relationships in Israel. In
         Transaction and Meaning: Directions in the
         Anthropology of Exchange and Symbolic Behavior, pp.
         226-75. B. Kapferer, ed. Philadelphia: Institute
         for the Study of Human Issues.

Heginbotham, Stanley J.
  1975   Cultures in Conflict: The Four Faces of the Indian
         Bureaucracy. New York: Columbia University Press.

Hettiarachchy, Tilak
  1972   History of Kingship in Ceylon. Colombo: Lake House.

Hoselitz, Bert F.
  1963   Levels of Economic Performance and Bureaucratic
         Structures. In Bureaucracy and Political Development,
         pp. 168-98. Joseph LaPalombara, ed. Princeton:
         Princeton University Press.

Huessler, Robert
  1963   Yesterday's Rulers: The Making of the British
         Colonial Service. Syracuse: Syracuse University
         Press.

Kannagara, P.D.
  1966   The History of the Ceylon Civil Service, 1802-1833.
         Dehiwela: Tissara Press.

Katz, E. and B. Danet
  1966   Petitions and Persuasive Appeals: A Study of Official
         Client Relations. American Sociological Review
         31:811-22.

Katz, E. and S.N. Eisenstadt
  1965   Some Sociological Observations on the Response of
         Israeli Organizations to New Immigrants. In Essays on
         Comparative Institutions, pp. 251-71. S.N.
         Eisenstadt, ed. New York: John Wiley & Sons.

Kearney, Robert N.
  1969   Ceylon: The Contemporary Bureaucracy. In Asian
         Bureaucratic Systems Emergent from the British
         Imperial Tradition, pp. 485-549. R. Braibanti, ed.
         Durham: Duke University Press.

Leitan, G.R. Tressie
  1979   Local Government and Decentralized Administration in
         Sri Lanka. Colombo: Lake House.

Leys, Colin
    1965   What Is the Problem about Corruption? The Journal of
            Modern African Studies 3(2):215-30.

Marx, Emmanuel.
    1972   Some Social Contexts of Personal Violence. In The
            Allocation of Responsibility. Max Gluckman, ed.
            Manchester: Manchester University Press.

Mauss, Marcel
    1966   The Gift. Ian Cunnison, trans. London: Cohen & West.

Mead, George H.
    1934   Mind, Self and Society. Edited, and with an
            Introduction by Charles W. Morris. Chicago: The
            University of Chicago Press.

Mendis, G.C.
    1956   The Colebrooke-Cameron Papers: Documents on British
            Colonial Policy in Ceylon, 1796-1833. Bombay: Oxford
            University Press.

Merton, Robert K.
    1965   Bureaucratic Structure and Personality. In Social
            Theory and Social Structure, pp. 195-206. New York:
            Free Press.

Obeyesekere, Gananath
    1982   Medusa's Hair. Chicago: The University of Chicago
            Press.

Parsons, Talcott
    1962   Categories of the Orientation and Organization of
            Action. In Toward a General Theory of Action, pp.
            53-109. Talcott Parsons and Edward Shils, eds. New
            York: Harper and Row.

Pieris, Ralph
    1956   Sinhalese Social Organization: The Kandyan Period.
            Colombo: The Ceylon University Press.

Pressman, Jeffrey L. and Aaron Wildavsky
    1979   Implementation: How Great Expectations in Washington
            Are Dashed in Oakland; or, Why It's Amazing that
            Federal Programs Work at All. Berkeley: The
            University of California Press.

Presthus, R.V.
    1962   Weberian vs. Welfare Bureaucracy in Traditional
            Society. Administrative Science Quarterly 6:1-24.

186

Price, Robert M.
    1975   Society and Bureaucracy in Contemporary Ghana.
           Berkeley: The University of California Press.

Riggs, Fred W.
    1958   Bazaar -- Canteen Moden.   Philippine Sociological
           Review 3:6-59.

    1961   The Ecology of Public Administration.   New Delhi:
           Asia Publishing House.

    1966   Thailand: The Modernization of a Bureaucratic Polity.
           Honolulu: East-West Center Press.

    1970   Frontiers of Development Administration.   Durham:
           University of North Carolina Press.

Roethlisbeger, F.J. and W.J. Dickson
    1939   Management and the Worker.   Cambridge: Harvard
           University Press.

Samaraweera, Vijaya
    1975   The Role of the Bureaucracy.   The Ceylon Journal of
           Historical and Social Studies IV(1-2):31-39.

Saparamadu, S.D.
    1960   Introduction to Leonard Woolf's Diaries in Ceylon,
           1908-1911.   Ceylon Historical Journal 9(1-4):vii-xlv.

Schwartz, Barry
    1975   Queuing and Waiting.   Studies in the Social
           Organization of Access and Delay.   Chicago: The
           University of Chicago Press.

Siffin, William J.
    1966   The Thai Bureaucracy: Institutional Change and
           Development.   Honolulu: East-West Center Press.

Spiro, Herbert J.
    1962   Politics in Africa.   Englewood Cliffs: Prentice Hall.

Sri Lanka, Government of
    1972   Department of Census and Statistics.   Census of
           Population 1971:   Preliminary Report.   Colombo.

    n.d.   Department of National Archives.   Lot Numbers 26/206,
           27/274.   Colombo.

    n.d.   Government Agents' Workshop (1975).   Report on the
           District Political Authority System.   Colombo.

    1954   Public Service Commission.   Report.   Colombo.

Sun
1976   King Peons. (June 9) Colombo: Independent
        Newspapers.

Taub, Richard P.
1969   Bureaucrats under Stress: Administrators and
        Administration in an Indian State. Berkeley: The
        University of California Press.

Tennent, Sir James E.
1859   Ceylon: Account of the Island, Physical, Historical
        and Topographical. Vol. 2. London: Longman, Green,
        Longman, and Roberts.

Toussaint, J.R.
1935   Annals of the Ceylon Civil Service. Colombo:
        Apothecaries Press.

Weber, Max
1968   Economy and Society 3. Guenther Roth and Claus
        Wittich, eds. New York: Bedminster Press.

1969a   Objectivity in Social Science and Social Policy. In
        The Methodology of the Social Sciences, pp. 49-112.
        Edited and translated by Edward A. Shils and Henry A.
        Finch. New York: Free Press.

1969b   The Theory of Social and Economic Organiaation.
        Talcott Parsons, ed. New York: Free Press.

1973   From Max Weber: Essays in Sociology. Hans H. Gerth
        and C. Wright Mills, eds. New York: Oxford
        University Press.

Wertheim, W.F.
1965   Sociological Aspects of Corruption in South East Asia.
        In East-West Parallels, pp. 105-25. The Hague:
        Van Hoeve.

Wickremeratne, L.A.
1970   The Rulers and the Ruled in British Ceylon: A Study
        of the Functions of Petitions in Colonial Governments.
        Modern Ceylon Studies: A Journal of the Social
        Sciences 1(2):213-32.

Wiswa Warnapala, W.A.
1974   Civil Service Administration in Ceylon: A Study in
        Bureaucratic Adaptation. Sri Lanka: Department of
        Government Printing.

Woodruff, Philip
1954   The Men Who Ruled India. London: Jonathan Cape.

Woolf, Leonard
   1962 <u>Diaries</u> <u>in</u> <u>Ceylon</u>, <u>1908</u>-<u>1911</u>. S.D. Saparamadu, ed.
       Colombo: Metro Press.

   1967 <u>Growing</u>: <u>An</u> <u>Autobiography</u> <u>of</u> <u>the</u> <u>Years</u> <u>1904</u>-<u>1911</u>.
       London: Hogarth Press.

Note on the Author

Namika Raby is a political anthropologist who teaches on comparative politics, political culture, and South Asia in the Department of Political Science, University of California, San Diego. Funded by a Foreign Area Fellowship of the Social Science Research Council and the American Council of Learned Societies, she researched regional administration in Sri Lanka during 1976-77. She has written on the topic of bureaucracy in the politics of meaning, the role of the administrator and the politician in Sri Lankan development, and kinship as ideology in the mediation of conflict within a bureaucratic setting in Sri Lanka. As a participant in the 1984 NASA Summer Workshop, she researched the cultural dimensions of the exercise of power and authority among multinational teams in outer space, and is the author of an article on "space culture" to be published by NASA/Johnson Space Center.